D0458688

Top Talent

MEMO TO THE CEO

Authored by leading experts and examining issues of special urgency, the books in the Memo to the CEO series are tailored for today's time-starved executives. Concise, focused, and solutions-oriented, each book explores a critical management challenge and offers authoritative counsel, provocative points of view, and practical insight.

Manage the Media
(Don't Let the Media Manage You)
by William J. Holstein, award-winning writer for
the *New York Times*, *Fortune*, and *Barron's*

Reward Systems: Does Yours Measure Up?
by Steve Kerr, former CLO of General Electric
and Goldman Sachs

Strategic Alliances: Three Ways to Make Them Work
by Steve Steinhilber, Vice President of Strategic
Alliances at Cisco Systems

Succession: Are You Ready?
by Marshall Goldsmith, author of the best-selling book
What Got You Here Won't Get You There

Winning in Turbulence
by Darrell Rigby, Bain & Company, Inc.

Cut Costs, Grow Stronger
by Shumeet Banerji, Paul Leinwand, and Cesare
R. Mainardi, Booz & Company

Top Talent

*Keeping Performance Up
When Business Is Down*

Sylvia Ann Hewlett

Harvard Business Press
Boston, Massachusetts

"The Morning After" (from "The Poseidon Adventure"), words and music by
Al Kasha and Joel Hirschhorn © 1972 (renewed) WB Music Corp. &
Warner-Tamerlane Publishing Corp. All Rights Reserved. Used by Permission of
Alfred Publishing Co., Inc.

ISBN: 978-1-4221-4042-0

Library-of-Congress cataloging information forthcoming

The paper used in this publication meets the requirements of the American
National Standard for Permanence of Paper for Publications and Documents
in Libraries and Archives Z39.48-1992.

For Richard

Contents

Contents

Acknowledgments

This is a highly collaborative book so it gives me particular pleasure to acknowledge the extensive help I've received from colleagues and from the leaders of the Hidden Brain Drain Task Force.

I'm deeply grateful to Catherine Fredman for her valuable help—without her editorial skills and keen judgment I could not have cleared the hurdles involved in writing this fast track book. I'm also extremely appreciative of the efforts of my research team at the Center for Work-Life Policy—Diana Forster, Joanne Gordon, Shelley Haynes, Ripa Rashid, Laura Sherbin, Eytan Sosnovich, and Karen Sumberg. A special thanks to Peggy Shiller—who led the team and pulled out all the stops to ensure we hit the tough, tight deadlines.

In addition, I'm enormously grateful to Melinda Merino, my editor at the Harvard Business Press, Molly Friedrich, my longtime literary agent, and Courtney Schinke.

Finally, I owe a huge debt of gratitude to the business leaders who shaped this study. The senior executives who appear in the pages of this book had the guts and the vision to identify and wrestle with the painful but enormously important talent challenges thrown up by this Great Recession. It took courage and I thank you.

Introduction:
A Recession Is a
Terrible Thing to Waste

"Now more than ever before, we're counting on our best people to find new ways to drive growth in this brutal marketplace. Reaching out to support, sustain, and fully engage top talent is central to our strategy."

—Jeffrey B. Kindler,
Chairman and CEO, Pfizer

Every company has its constellation of stars—the consistent top performers who help the organization shine. Found at all levels, from associate to senior vice president, from analyst to managing director, stars are known for their outsized dedication, brainpower, and work ethic. They're the vital few who contribute the most to the bottom line and drive a company's results and reputation.

In these bleak times, companies are depending on their star performers as never before to light the way out of the darkness. Organizations need their top talent to be in peak form—firing on all cylinders—so that they can succeed in a market that is the toughest in living memory.

How are employers handling this challenge?

In a word, badly.

To start with, leaders are seriously distracted. Caught between clamoring customers and vaporizing value, a CEO understandably might find it hard to focus on talent. People strategies tend to translate into layoff strategies: how many should you let go? How should the cuts be distributed? Should you act surgically and strike deep, or should you dribble out the reductions over time?

When it comes to talent management, CEOs are also hamstrung by outmoded thinking. In times like these—marked by massive losses and rising unemployment—it's tempting to imagine that there's no need to worry about motivating talent. People are so grateful to have a job, the conventional thinking goes, that they can be relied to contribute 110 percent. Right?

Wrong.

Cutting-edge research from the Center for Work-Life Policy's Hidden Brain Drain Task Force (which

comprises fifty of the world's most powerful corporations, including Ernst & Young, General Electric,
Goldman Sachs, Intel, Johnson & Johnson, Siemens,
and Unilever) reveals the danger in conventional
assumptions about sustaining high performance in
tough times. Consider these crucial and disturbing
data points:

- In the wake of a reduction in force (RIF)—a
  popular euphemism for mass layoffs—voluntary attrition can be deeper than the RIF itself.
  A Center for Work-Life Policy (CWLP) survey
  shows that between June 2008 and January 2009,
  14 percent of college graduates lost their jobs
  —of these, 32 percent were fired, but another
  68 percent voluntarily left their jobs. In a similar vein, a recent University of Wisconsin study
  showed that 31 percent of survivors walk out
  the door in the wake of a layoff—many of
  them the star performers companies most
  needed to keep. Participants in Hidden Brain
  Drain strategy sessions were brutally honest
  when commenting on the impact of the current round of RIFs: a large percentage were
  looking to quit; 64 percent were considering
  leaving, and 24 percent were spending most
  of their time actively looking for another job.

- Those who stay report feeling disengaged, of being caught in long term limbo: 74 percent of participants talked about being paralyzed, 73 percent felt demoralized, and 64 percent felt demotivated. "It seems pointless to overcommit to work since the company does not seem to commit to its employees," commented one participant.

- Interestingly, the flight risk is highest for women, with twice as many women as men considering leaving and many others actively looking for the next job.

The research presented in this book tells a disturbing story. It seems that in troubled times, companies routinely compound their problems by ignoring and neglecting star performers—taking them for granted. And we're not talking only about the top of the house (the C-suite); we're talking about high-potential and high-performing employees at every level and rank.

The data is chilling: loyalty is out the window, engagement has fallen off a cliff, and large numbers of top performers are angry, alienated, and looking to quit. Far from lighting the way forward, many stellar producers have one foot out the door. They feel sidelined and sideswiped by bosses intent on other agendas.

Some leaders see the flashing red lights. "We need our top talent more than ever," says Jeffrey L. Bewkes, chairman and CEO of Time Warner. "Creating media and entertainment that appeals to consumers is much more difficult in the current economic environment. We need to hold on to our best."

Other leaders ignore the danger signals—to the company's detriment.

This book underscores the fact that these are treacherous times on the talent retention front. Standout performers always have options, even in tough times. Indeed it's precisely in tough times that competitors poach your best people. "This is a brilliant time for talent acquisition," notes Carolyn Buck Luce, global life sciences sector leader at Ernst & Young.

When stars leave in more buoyant times, companies can often find a way to replace them, either by luring high performers from other organizations or by taking the time to groom successors. But in an economic quagmire, many companies lack the luxury of spare time or money. In troubled times, when the stars go out they leave a dark void.

In early 2008, the Hidden Brain Drain Task Force decided to engage with these challenges.[1] As the credit crisis deepened, fourteen task force companies (American Express, Bloomberg, Booz Allen Hamilton, Booz & Company, Citi, Credit Suisse, Ernst & Young,

General Electric, Goldman Sachs, Lehman Brothers, Merrill Lynch, Moody's, Time Warner, and UBS) helped us reach high-potential employees across a range of sectors to explore the impact of the market turndown on the sustainability of talent on both Wall Street and Main Street. Central to the investigation were questions such as, How do managers maintain loyalty in the face of massive layoffs? How do managers sustain performance in the face of dwindling compensation? What can managers do to reduce flight risk and rekindle commitment?

The research (designed and executed by a team from the Center for Work-Life Policy), started with an analysis of Hidden Brain Drain data on high-echelon jobs, which created a 2006 baseline.[2] The team then layered on data from a series of virtual strategy sessions conducted in June and December 2008.[3] The findings allow us to compare 2006 (a time of boom and ebullient profits) with June 2008 (a time of credit crunch and falling growth rates) with December 2008 (a time of gut-wrenching economic meltdown). A detailed research report with additional data is available from the Harvard Business Press.[4]

The data analysis phase of the research was followed—in January through March 2009—with a series of fifty-five targeted, one-on-one interviews. CEOs, C-suite executives, talent managers, and high-potential talent across a range of sectors and geographies were asked to react to our findings and respond to the following questions. How can top performers be pulled out of this state of long-term limbo and reengage? How can they be motivated to give their best once again?

The result is powerful: a menu of pragmatic interventions that outlines how companies can do a much better job of managing talent in troubled times. Here they are in a nutshell:

- Create a "no-spin" zone.

- Think locally, and focus on team leaders.

- Give employees meaningful nonmonetary rewards.

- Develop a fair restructuring process.

- Hold on to your women.

- Show that top leadership cares.

- Re-create pride, purpose, and direction.

- P.S. Don't forget yourself.

The good news: there are plenty of effective ways to tend to top talent that do not involve spending money. In fact, *only* spending money doesn't have a long-lasting impact and may do more harm than good, because it lulls leaders into thinking that a big bonus compensates for bad behavior. As the Beatles reminded us, "Money can't buy me love." One advantage of tough times: in place of the easy palliative of a souped-up paycheck, managers must turn to alternatives that truly satisfy employees' needs and wants.

When things were going well, companies could afford to spend heedlessly in the talent wars. But when every dollar counts, leaders are forced to define explicitly what is necessary to delight customers, serve clients, and motivate talent—in short, to identify the real levers of value.

We live and work in a knowledge-based era, in which the drivers of value are not machines but brains. Staying ahead of the competition is no longer about knocking out widgets; rather, it's about making the most of high-octane brainpower.

Talent is the gift that keeps on giving. It's self-regenerating. If you invest in talent, the returns will be exponential and lasting. In 2009, retaining, sustaining, and fully realizing top talent are the keys to renewal and growth.

A recession is a terrible thing to waste. There are powerful opportunities in tough times to create a richer talent management model. Born in adversity, it will carry your organization into prosperity—and keep you there for years to come.

PART I

The Evidence

The Top Talent Challenge

In 2006, Anne Erni was in love—with her job. "I was in an organization that really valued what I was doing," recalls the former chief diversity officer of Lehman Brothers. "I was getting so much positive feedback from every part of the firm. It was such an amazing adrenaline rush."

That rush carried Erni through workweeks that involved back-to-back meetings followed by eleven-hour days when, she says, "I would have to deliver what I promised in those meetings." At least one night a week, Erni had a speaking engagement or a professional dinner to attend, and at least one night, she stayed at work until midnight and then faced the commute back to New Jersey, her husband, and two kids.

Her hefty paycheck only reinforced her dedication. "Every year my pay went up—sometimes significantly. I knew that the more I worked, the more I got done, the more I earned. So that drove me, too."

A year later, the first rumblings of the coming cataclysm began to shake the financial industry and the layoffs began. Erni's boss and mentor stepped down. By July 2007, Erni's budget had been slashed to the bare amount necessary to cover commitments. "It wasn't about being proactive anymore; it was just about getting by," she says.

A second round of layoffs ensued. By August 2008, Erni was starting to question the viability of the job she had adored. "The pain of seeing everything come apart all around me was really hard to bear. For the first time in my career, I started to get disillusioned."

Erni stopped working long hours, and, once she began to spend more time at home, "I realized how much I had *not* been doing for my family. I hadn't gone on my son's field trips, I had delegated a lot. And I thought, 'Oh, my god, what did I miss?'"

Lehman Brothers filed for bankruptcy in September 2008. Erni was laid off in November, and by that time the joy of her work had drained along with her 401(k) account.

The Talent Time Bomb

Anne Erni's trajectory, it turns out, is typical—not only of the financial industry, with its outsized demands and outsized rewards, but also of high-potential employees in every sector.

When the Center for Work-Life Policy's Hidden Brain Drain Task Force first began to study top performers in 2006, it was a heady time, with the global economy firing on all cylinders. Strategic planning committees routinely asked not whether to expand but how much. There was a sense among top performers that limitless rewards were within reach if they only stretched a little further.

The concern that dominated our study was a simple one: how far was top talent willing—or able—to stretch before reaching the breaking point? In a series of surveys and focus groups, we targeted professionals who worked at least sixty hours per week, were in the top 6 percent earnings bracket, and held positions with at least five of the following performance pressures: unpredictable workload; fast-paced work with tight deadlines; work-related events outside regular hours; 24/7 availability to clients; a great deal of travel; a scope of work that amounted to more than one job; responsibility for profit and loss; responsibility for recruiting and mentoring; a great many direct reports; more than ten hours a day of face time; and insufficient staffing. This elite group—think of them as the Delta Force of the workplace—comprised men and women of all ages and at all stages of their careers employed in a wide range of industries. We explored why they loved their jobs, what motivated them to work so hard, what personal goals they were willing to trade for professional success, and whether that success was ultimately worth the sacrifices.

Our findings described a balancing act, a reciprocal deal. Top talent was willing to pull out all the stops—work seventy-hour weeks and cope with a myriad of performance pressures—as long as companies came through with rich rewards: intellectual challenge, recognition, and comp packages to die for. In other words, companies were able to hold on to these engines of productivity and growth as long as companies ponied up the goods.

We concluded that the top talent model was "in equilibrium." This model had tensions and flaws, which particularly impacted women, but by and large it was working. In the ebullient, expansive world of 2006, the rewards of top jobs were outsize enough to justify the outsize effort they required. Little did we know we were sitting on a talent time bomb. Shortly after we completed the study, the subprime mortgage crisis triggered a brutal economic downturn. There were knock-on effects everywhere.

Spurred by these distressing events, we revisited the talent model in the period of March to July 2008, when the first ominous tremors were beginning to shake the global economy, and again in December 2008, when the foundations had shattered. From Wall Street to

FIGURE 1

The talent time bomb: loyalty, trust, and engagement fall off a cliff

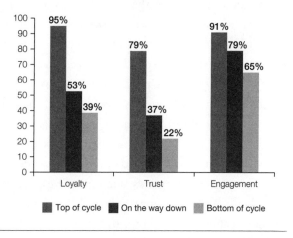

Main Street, top performers' loyalty, trust, and engagement had fallen steeply. Figure 1 shows what happened at seven Wall Street firms at the epicenter of the crisis. For top talent, the reciprocal deal was over.

What would it take to pick up the pieces? Would it even be possible?

The View from the Top of the Cycle

In 2006, the most salient finding was how much top performers loved their jobs. They loved the intellectual challenge and the thrill of achieving difficult goals. They loved the stimulation of smart colleagues and the camaraderie of a well-tuned team. They were addicted to the adrenaline rush of the next tough assignment. Far from seeing themselves as overworked drones, they wore their commitments like a badge of honor. Two-thirds of survey respondents in our study said that the pressure and the pace of their jobs were self-inflicted. Although clearly they were aware of the toll their jobs took on their lives outside the office, most of the high achievers felt that the sacrifices—as well as the stress and strain—were justified by the rich rewards.

What were these rewards, and how did top talent rank them? A large majority stressed the challenge and stimulation of the work; this was the top pick for men as well as women. Compensation, recognition, status, "meaning and purpose," and flex options were also important motivators. Interestingly, money wasn't the prime driver. It was important but not dominant. As shown in figure 2, less than half (40 percent) of respondents in our surveys rated high levels of compensation as the main reason they loved their jobs. Only in the financial sector, with its tradition of outsized bonuses, did that figure edge over the 50 percent mark (56 percent).

Note that among female top talent, monetary rewards were trumped by four other factors. In focus

FIGURE 2

Why top performers love their jobs

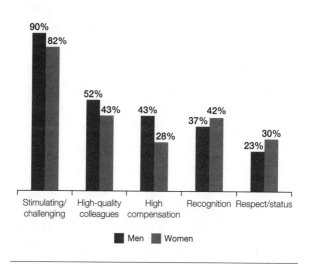

groups high-performing women (and at least some men) talked about the importance of respect and recognition—from bosses and companies—and the satisfaction they derived from working with a group of great colleagues.

Whatever the complexities of the motivational map, the outsize efforts expended by this Delta Force of the workplace came at a huge personal cost. Our surveys revealed that men and women alike were teetering on the brink of a cliff. Their overdrive work model was taking a toll on their personal and family lives—even their sex lives—to a degree that threatened their well-being. A significant number (59 percent) of survey respondents said that work pressures were undermining their health, and 40 percent felt that their jobs were undermining their relationships with spouses or partners. Women felt the pain especially keenly. Although men and women perceived the stress at work in much the same way, women were disproportionately tuned in to stress at home, seeing a direct link between their long workweeks and a variety of distressing behaviors in their children: watching too much television, eating too much junk food, underachieving in school, and acting out.

Men as well as women were aware that they were performing a delicate balancing act. The promise of significant payback—power and purpose as well as compensation—would keep them in harness for a number of years, but down the road a significant minority of these high-echelon professionals wanted to trade in their jobs for something less stressful.

The View from the Bottom of the Cycle

Then, in 2008, the financial crisis and economic collapse tore through the top talent model like a hurricane.

The most sobering finding of our 2008 research was that for high performers the joy of work evaporated overnight. In its place was an anxiety so pervasive that, as one strategy session participant reported, "At night I'm tossing and turning and grinding my teeth so badly that I've developed cracks in my molars." Hidden Brain Drain survey data shows that 50 percent of high-echelon workers have experienced at least one negative health effect as a result of the downturn.

Love for one's job—and, by extension, the organization—was being choked off by insecurity and betrayal. Compensation packages that relied on company stock options were a bitter pill to swallow, as swooning stock prices vaporized the accumulated rewards of years of hard work. The suddenness of the change was especially shocking. People reported losing their sense of balance—of equilibrium—as everything they had counted on was jarred out of place.

Respect and recognition gave way to a bunker mentality, with everyone fighting for a space in a small and insecure shelter. In an interview, a senior Wall Street executive talked about the corporate culture "turning tribal." Supervisors were busy placating frantic clients and figuring out whose job to cut in the next round of layoffs, leaving them little time to pay attention to their former stars, who inevitably felt neglected. Colleagues were too panic stricken or too busy trying to protect themselves to extend the camaraderie that formerly sparked ideas and made the workplace congenial. Teams were torn apart as head count was cut. Survivors facing threats to their own job security were shouldering heavy workloads (81 percent compared with 61 percent a year earlier) and coping with tremendous face-time pressure (55 percent compared with 22 percent a year earlier), and that forced them to put in even longer hours. (Hidden Brain Drain January 2009 survey data shows that 22 percent of high-echelon workers are now working an extra nine hours a week.)

In this punishing work environment, loyalty, trust, and engagement have almost evaporated. With star status no longer a guarantee of respect, job security, or compensation, the number of employees on Wall Street who trust their organizations plunged from 79 percent in June 2007 to 22 percent in December 2008; on Main Street, it sank from 85 percent to 56 percent over the same time period. Loyalty has also plummeted, falling from 95 percent to 39 percent on Wall Street, and from 88 percent to 71 percent on Main Street. The figures on engagement levels are particularly disturbing, dropping from 91 percent to 65 percent on Wall Street, and from a nearly perfect 97 percent to a middling 85 percent on Main Street.

The survivors of the RIFs (reductions in force) are having a hard time focusing on the work at hand. When participants in Hidden Brain Drain strategy sessions were asked to tell us the first word that came to mind when describing their current work environment, they said, "thankless," "chaotic," "stressful," "frustrating," "overwhelming and unsustainable," "depressing," and just plain "sad."

Strategy session participants described the level of stress generated by the economic downturn as "physically and mentally crippling." Nearly eight of ten participants reported extremely high levels of stress, more than twice the number as one year earlier, with symptoms ranging from ulcers and migraine headaches to a new dependence on sleep medication. Typical comments included "I can't focus on work—I'm too distracted by tensions in my gutted team and worries about my job" and "I probably should be working out, but given the relentless bad news, all I can deal with at the end of a stress-filled day is a stiff drink."

As employees struggled to cope, negative strategies—such as taking sleeping pills, drinking, smoking, biting one's nails, overeating, and losing one's temper—trumped positive ways of coping. Work-related stress transformed Dr. Jekylls into Mr. Hydes, as parents reported "yelling at the kids more than I like" and spouses noted "more stupid fighting." In June 2007, 30 percent of respondents were struggling with eating issues and 23 percent with drinking issues. One year later these figures had risen appreciably, to 41 percent and 30 percent, respectively. Weight issues were also on the rise, with respondents saying, "I would love to [exercise regularly] but I just don't have time." Not very long ago, high-octane jobs made members of the workplace Delta Force feel special and worthwhile, but now these same jobs were turning them into people they didn't know and didn't like.

Key Facts

Loyalty, Trust, and Engagement

- On Wall Street, loyalty has plummeted from 95 percent in June 2007 to 39 percent in December 2008. On Main Street, loyalty fell from 88 percent to 71 percent.

- Trust has plunged from 79 percent to 22 percent on Wall Street over the same period; and from 85 percent to 56 percent on Main Street.

- Engagement on Wall Street has dropped from 91 percent to 65 percent. On Main Street, it has fallen from 97 percent to 85 percent.

Body Blows and Fallout in Personal Life

- 59 percent of respondents said that work pressures were undermining their health (65 percent on Wall Street).

- 40 percent felt their jobs were undermining their relationship with spouses or partners (50 percent on Wall Street).

- 78 percent of high-echelon workers reported experiencing high levels of stress, more than twice as high as one year earlier.

- Symptoms range from "crashing" at the end of the day (70 percent versus 43 percent six months earlier) to an "emptied out" sex life (37 percent versus 30 percent six months earlier).

Key Pressure Points

- Survivors of layoffs experience heavier workloads (81 percent compared to 61 percent one year earlier) and tremendous face-time pressure (55 percent compared to 22 percent).

- In January 2009, 22 percent of high-echelon workers report working an average of nine extra hours per week compared to six months earlier.

Men, Women, and Flight Risk

- 64 percent of Wall Street survivors and 41 percent of Main Street employees were considering leaving their current companies.

- Twice as many women as men on Wall Street (84 percent compared to 40 percent) were considering leaving their employers.

- Fewer than a quarter (22 percent) of women who had "one foot out the door" in December 2008 planned to take time out of the workforce.

Disengagement on Wall Street

- Employees in the financial sector reported feeling paralyzed (74 percent), demoralized (73 percent), and demotivated (64 percent).

One Foot Out the Door

When top talent feels this way it's bad news for any organization. CEOs cannot blithely assume that valued employees will be so grateful for a job—any job—that they'll put in the hours and the effort no matter how bad the working conditions are. There are two serious risks: top performers will walk away (and competitors are always on the prowl for proven producers), or they will settle in to what one strategy session participant called "long-term limbo," clinging to a steady paycheck but tamping down commitment. In the words of another participant, "I quit but stayed on the job."

How serious is the flight risk? Recent research shows it to be more substantial than expected. A *Harvard Business Review* article (May 2008) shows attrition after a layoff to be much deeper than the layoff itself: in this study 31 percent of survivors walked out the door in the wake of a relatively modest layoff. Hidden Brain Drain strategy sessions also uncovered significant flight risk; 64 percent of survivors on Wall Street were considering leaving, and 24 percent were actively looking for a job. Among these, 35 percent anticipated going to a competitor, 29 percent wanted to switch to a less risky industry, and 15 percent were planning to start their own businesses. "The loyalty of the institution to its people, and vice versa, isn't really there anymore—it's a different animal from what a lot of us were used to," muses a partner at a white-shoe New York law firm that recently announced it would lay off two hundred lawyers. "The problem is we're supposed to all be in this together. But at some point, you stop and think: 'Well, maybe we're not.'"

Interestingly, in this downturn, flight risk continues to be differentiated by gender. Strategy session data revealed that twice as many women as men were considering leaving their employers, and many more women than men were actively looking for another job. In a way, that's not surprising: women are constantly recalibrating at the margin, calculating whether the professional benefits of their jobs outweigh the costs. In the words of one woman, "When I walk out the door in the morning, leaving my two-year-old with the babysitter, there's usually a bit of a scene. Tommy clings, pouts, and whips up the guilt. Now, I know it's not serious—most of the time he likes his sitter. But it sure makes me think about why I go to work—and why I put in a ten-hour day. It's as though every day I make the following calculation: do the satisfactions I derive from my job (efficacy, recognition—a sense of stretching my mind) justify leaving Tommy? These days it's a close run."

Recalibrating at the margin is encouraged by the fact that a significant minority of high-performing women (31 percent) are married to men who earn more than they do, and therefore they can choose whether to work. All this explains why, in difficult times, more women than men are likely to head for the door.

If flight risk is a serious problem for companies, how serious are plummeting rates of engagement and "long-run limbo"?

The data shows distressing levels of disengagement. In our strategy sessions, 73 percent of participants reported feeling "demoralized," 74 percent felt "paralyzed," and 64 percent felt "demotivated." Even top performers were no longer hitting previous highs. "I want to be engaged, but with things in chaos it's hard to lock on to purpose," said one participant who had a track record as a top producer. Another commented, "I am just not as pumped as I used to be in the mornings. There's more dread than excitement about the day ahead."

It's clear that in the current environment many employees—even high-performing ones—feel they need to cling to a steady paycheck, but participants in our strategy sessions were honest about the impact of the current negative work environment on morale and productivity. "I feel betrayed. Five years of extraordinary effort just went down the drain. And no one seems to care—least of all my immediate boss. It's easy to get cynical—to dial down and tune out—to focus on looking after number one."

Still, plenty of the strategy session participants recognize that challenging times present opportunities for their organizations and for their own professional advancement. More important, they know exactly what it takes to recharge their energies.

PART II

What to Do About It

1: Create a "No-Spin" Zone

You're sitting in an airplane stuck on the tarmac. What would you want to hear from the flight deck?

David Eun, vice president of strategic partnerships at Google, knows what he'd do if he were the pilot. Instead of waiting until he had detailed information on when the plane would take off, he would get on the airplane intercom system. He would apologize to the passengers for the delay, share what he was being told by the control tower, and tell them what his experience suggested might happen next. He would keep it brief and to the point, and then promise to update them regularly. He would then do just that, even if he had no new information to share.

"I wouldn't pretend to know exactly how or when the situation would be resolved, or imagine I could give them information they'd necessarily like," says Eun. But, he says, passengers would still breathe a sigh of relief because he'd have provided *some* information.

Keeping people informed, resetting expectations as relevant, and consistently meeting those reset expectations can empower and reassure people who are otherwise unable to change the situation they're in. Communicating directly and honestly shows them they are top of mind and that the person in charge respects their ability to understand the situation they—and he—are in together. This transparency reflects a different kind of leadership, based on the concept of acknowledging the accountability of leaders to their employees—and proactively accepting responsibility for things within the control of leadership—without providing false hope.

In troubled times, many managers tend to hunker down behind closed doors, until they have definitive answers or can shift the blame to other people or forces beyond their control. Others tend to give vague assurances that they think people want to hear, to make them "feel better," even if it isn't clear such assurances are warranted. That's the opposite of what's needed.

Participants in Hidden Brain Drain strategy sessions told us that undercommunicating is a greater risk than overcommunicating. Everyone's anxiety level is already off the charts; silence from those supposedly in the know only makes it worse. When leaders don't provide information, even the prized people whose positions seem safe start second-guessing what's going on. The resulting rumor mill inevitably undermines trust. "You have to have the courage to talk, even if it's just to say, 'We don't know,'" says Kathryn Quigley, head of Americas talent management at Credit Suisse. "But whatever you do, you must say something, because people interpret saying nothing as meaning something bad."

And whatever you say, make sure it's honest. "The idea that you can manage communications and spin the truth is pretty much wishful thinking," says Tom Stewart, chief marketing and knowledge officer for consulting firm Booz & Company. In the age of the Internet, companies cannot avoid or cover up difficult facts. Rest assured that your employees will obsessively root out the smallest snippets of new information and broadcast them in real time via BlackBerry, cell phone, and Twitter. Trust can be built and maintained only through transparency: leaders at all levels must commit to a "no-spin" zone.

Calling All Managers

Effective communication in times of crisis involves all levels of management. According to participants in Hidden Brain Drain strategy sessions, "Not just the CEO but all managers need to be more 'open book,' so that people understand the realities of the situation." Still, hearing from senior leaders might be particularly helpful.

"It is critical that employees hear from the most senior ranks of management," says Frances G. Laserson, president of The Moody's Foundation and former vice president of corporate communications, Moody's Corporation. "They have the thirty-thousand-foot view of where the company sits in the overall economy. That's something a lower-level manager can't supply." But, Laserson adds, "Best practice in a company is for senior management to provide talking points for individual managers and supervisors. Employees prefer to get their information from their immediate manager. Team leaders are the most believable source of information."

Neither top management nor immediate supervisors will have credibility with employees, however, if their messages are contradictory. At networking giant Cisco, global manager meetings are scheduled for the day before quarterly performance announcements. This practice gives leaders a chance to hear and understand corporate messaging and prepare for questions from their employees.

To ensure that information cascades throughout the organization consistently, you should make sure that before any important announcement all managers receive a series of talking points providing detailed answers to specific questions. The points should cover items that people are most anxious about—for example, How will this news affect our company? What changes will occur as a result? What will that mean for me and my colleagues? How and when are things going to happen?

Choose the Right Medium for Your Message

Politicians and marketing experts know that it takes an average of eight sightings (or viewings) for an advertisement's message to sink in. And that's in ordinary times when people are distracted by normal things. This is no ordinary time. These days, members of your Delta Force or *A* team are likely to be more distracted than usual by concerns about keeping their jobs and making their mortgage payments. Thus managers need to use every tool at their disposal to engage the attention of top performers and keep them focused on the job at hand.

Luckily there's a wide spectrum of possibilities, ranging from town hall meetings to one-on-one conversations, with interesting options in between. Technology—videoconferencing, Webcasts, team and leader blogs, even Twitter—certainly helps create a sense of collaboration and camaraderie, and it should be part of ongoing communication efforts. These new forms of communication are especially important if you want to reinforce connectivity between global leaders, as pharmaceutical giant Pfizer discovered in a recent Webcast.

On March 9, 2009, Pfizer celebrated International Women's Day with a Webcast led by CEO Jeffrey Kindler and a group of top female leaders. They wanted to share information about new programs that seek to accelerate the careers of women in this science-based company. Five hundred high-potential Pfizer women from around the world logged on to the program, and many of them chose to participate in a lively Q&A with senior leaders. As Sandra Bushby, director of global diversity and inclusion, describes the event, "In turbulent times, this is a great way of cementing community—and giving voice to women around the world."

In a similar vein, EMC, a $14 billion technology organization based in Hopkinton, Massachusetts, uses social media to encourage "enterprise collaboration." On a internal social network called EMC ONE, EMC's forty thousand worldwide employees are encouraged to brainstorm new ideas and connect with one another in more than 160 virtual communities—such as one called "The Water Cooler"—where employees can collaborate on anything from green IT, to understanding the real-time competitive climate, to ways to celebrate the company's upcoming 30th anniversary, or simply to share what's on their minds.

Anyone at the company—from the CEO to engineers in Korea—can log on to the discussions. Like a virtual hallway, the "Water Cooler" community recognizes the power of unexpected conversations—thus it's both strategic and a way to connect people.

These conversations yield potential solutions to the special challenges of recession—from customized client services to cost savings—as employees swap experiences and expertise. In December 2008, one EMC employee posted a discussion on Water Cooler titled "Constructive Ideas to Save Money," which, as of May 2009, yielded over 23,000 hits and generated over 320 ideas for cost savings from EMC employees globally. Among the cost-saving ideas, employees suggested that the company offer unpaid time off and lower the temperature at EMC headquarters by two degrees—a suggestion that included a calculation of potential savings. "There were hundreds of very tangible cost-saving ideas that went above and beyond any ideas the company might have come up with," says Polly Pearson, vice president of employment brand and strategy development.

The Power of One-on-One

The best way to keep your prized people engaged is to keep in touch. Get out from behind the barricade of your desk and walk around, visiting workstations and offices. This practice counters the bunker mentality that people fall into under stress.

Even good managers need to be reminded to communicate more than usual during times of crisis. "Everyone's overloaded and on overdrive," reports Judith Nocito, assistant general counsel at manufacturing giant Alcoa. "You get so busy with urgent stuff that needs to be done that it helps to be reminded to just sit down and tell your group, 'Here's where we are now; you're not impacted today, and you're doing a great job.' Just hearing that can be very reassuring, rather than have people wondering what's going on."

You can further reassure employees by expanding the number of people you reach out to directly. Not only does this reinforce a sense of camaraderie, but it also reduces the risk of information getting garbled as it's passed along. At Time Warner, Lisa Quiroz, senior vice president of corporate responsibility, used to hold weekly meetings with six of her twenty-one staffers. In February 2008, she had to lay off one-third of her staff. Today, she holds weekly meetings with her entire group of twelve. "We did this because it is an easy way to connect with everyone, and it reduced redundant meetings," Quiroz says. "Sometimes, it is tough to get the right information from one level to the next because some managers are better communicators than others. Now, with everyone having increased responsibilities—as a result of staff cuts—this was also a good way to make everyone feel part of the team."

When crunched budgets limit travel, a new challenge becomes how to communicate one-on-one with top talent located on the other side of the country—or the world. Don't ignore the obvious: the most effective mode of communication is still picking up the phone and talking to far-flung colleagues. If one of your top performers works in a distant time zone, schedule regular one-on-one conversations and supplement them with IM pings. Leaders of virtual teams who drive to work can use their morning and evening commutes to connect with direct reports in various parts of the globe; in turn, direct reports should know that the rush hour may well be a good time for an uninterrupted conversation.

The bottom line: instead of having people piece together facts and figures from random sources and make their own interpretations, bring accurate information directly to them.

Listen Up!

Ultimately, what matters most is not where or how people connect but that they do connect.

Remember that the manager's job is not only to talk but also to listen. One way to drive high rates of employee engagement is to hold instigative (two-way rather than one-way) conversations—both to understand what's on people's minds and to re-create trust and community. Especially in tough times, managers should listen up and actively involve valued employees in decisions and changes rather than issue set-in-stone directives. Appearances are critical here. Reaching out to listen, showing by your actions that you value and respect the opinions of your colleagues, is a big step in the right direction.

Open the conversation to questions, and encourage people to share concerns as well as the latest rumors. At Moody's, companywide town hall meetings are followed immediately by mini-town halls between managers and their teams. Team leaders are instructed to ask, "Were your questions answered? What did you think? What are your concerns going forward?" They then pass the responses up and down the ladder. This sort of 360-degree involvement is especially valuable during difficult times, when even proven performers are likely to feel out of the loop and out of control.

Look for creative ways to link to people, to hear what they're thinking. Reach out to explain the rationale behind restructuring and any job reductions.

According to Alcoa's Nocito, "Constantly focusing on making sure people understand can take the sting out of the situation and lighten the mood of the doom and gloom. It's really important to keep people focused on things they can and should do—the things they can impact, rather than worrying about things outside of their control."

2: Think Locally and Focus on Team Leaders

Every year at performance review time, Steve Richardson, senior vice president (retired) for organizational capabilities at American Express, makes a small gesture that electrifies employees. He not only reads the performance reviews his direct reports write for their own direct reports but also includes a handwritten note on each review. "I personalize feedback for a wide group," he says. "Not only does this bolster individuals and their leaders, it shows that I care about what is happening several layers down in the organization."

It takes Richardson about ten minutes to read and comment on each of some eighty performance reviews, but he maintains that the payback is priceless. "I get thank-you notes and great feedback from people," he says, adding that one employee in Amsterdam e-mailed Richardson to say in his fifteen-year career at the company fifteen years he had never felt so touched.

"People join companies but leave managers," wrote authors Marcus Buckingham and Curt Coffman in *First, Break All the Rules* (New York: Simon & Schuster, 1999). An employee may join GE or Cisco or Goldman Sachs because she is lured by its generous benefits package and reputation for valuing employees. But Jeff Immelt, John Chambers, or Lloyd Blankfein and all the goodwill in the world can motivate her only so much. It is the employee's relationship with her immediate manager or team leaders that will determine how long she stays and how productive she is while she is there. In a down cycle, individual team leaders are the glue that holds the talent equation together.

Talented people who feel they're not appreciated by their immediate boss, who feel lost or confused in the economic storm, who don't trust their supervisors to get them through it, will leave at the earliest opportunity—and rest assured, long before they clean out their desks, their engagement will flag along with their productivity. The truism that managers trump companies is often brushed aside in good times; in tough times, organizations ignore it at their peril.

Love 'em or Lose 'em

We all know the phrase "blind panic." Since the economy began its sickening plunge, no one, not even your top talent, is immune to being too scared to think straight. Managers who can prevent their people from panicking are worth their weight in gold.

In tough times, people skills can be more critical to long-term success than strategic initiatives such as innovation or cost cutting. Commonsense practices, such as listening, empathizing, and coaching, are always valuable but never more so than during high-stress periods. You and your lieutenants can do a lot to strengthen team engagement just by showing a genuine sense of concern.

Paradoxically, these so-called soft skills often are muscled out by the hard realities of working under the gun. Without a conscious effort to emphasize the importance of people skills and contact points, many team leaders hunker down in their offices and isolate themselves. To be sure, good people skills can't be instilled overnight, but managers can and should be reminded of the importance of reaching out.

Susan Silbermann, currently regional president of Latin America for Pfizer, offers a simple way of ramping up touch points in these stressful times. With a team of two hundred people spread over several countries, she feels she doesn't have the bandwidth to cultivate close connections with every team member and needs a way to leverage everyone's— and especially her own—precious time. So last year she began holding monthly "birthday breakfasts." The framework is straightforward: once a month she invites everyone whose birthday falls that month to join her for an hour-long breakfast. As a result she has managed to meet and connect with most of her team in informal breakfast groups that cross the usual divides of gender, rank, and function and, as she says, "the ripple effect of holding these breakfasts has spread like wildfire." Morale and engagement has improved dramatically, and Silbermann has been able to solve a great many problems by the sheer act of connecting with a broader range of people. Impressively, Silbermann was able to do all this in about eighteen hours per year. That's a time commitment we can all aspire to.

Lynn Utter, president and COO of Knoll, tells us that what she loses sleep over is figuring out how she can better engage her talent in these difficult times. She has learned that a little goes a long way in this regard. Every week she e-mails four senior managers and asks them for the name of one person on their staff who has been exemplary. She then calls each person to thank him for his effort and congratulate him on a job well done. This practice has made a significant impact on performance across the company as her top performers understand that she appreciates their hard work and dedication. As Utter says, "If I can't make four phone calls a week to make this kind of difference, then I'm not doing my job."

Take Charge of Your Talent

In part I you learned that for top talent, the four most important motivators are challenge/stimulation, high-quality colleagues, recognition/respect, and compensation. You also learned that money is not the most important motivator. What then can team leaders do to strengthen the three other motivators so that top performers will disregard a slashed bonus or overlook the absence of a pay raise? Put yourself in the shoes of your high performers: in a year when comp packages are dwindling, what makes you want to pour yourself into your work?

High performers thrive on acing challenges and surpassing goals. In tough times, many of the performance measures set up in rosier days no longer apply. Asking your top performers to pursue them anyway only sets up your best people for failure and creates bitterness and distrust. Smart managers therefore channel team energy toward goals that are achievable in the current environment.

For example, it may be impossible for salespeople to meet the preceding year's quotas when half the market has suspended new purchases and customers have nixed product upgrades. When people cannot control external factors, you need to give them something they can control. This may mean shifting employees' performance goals from, for example, increasing revenue to reducing costs.

Don't assume that everyone on your team knows the most productive use of her time. Under stress, even talented people often make bad decisions about which projects to focus on and how. Many employees waste time, money, and energy on perceived priorities rather than on activities that make a real difference. You may have to become more of a micromanager to ensure that people are working not only hard but also smart.

Refocus your team on the tasks that matter, advises Adam Quinton, managing director and head of global macro research at Banc of America Securities Merrill Lynch. In his context that means servicing clients. "We don't know how long the downturn will go on or what the consequences will be, but helping clients and doing a great job is the best insurance policy for your career," Quinton tells his team. "If the worst happens, satisfied clients can be valuable sources of future employment opportunities in that they can provide contacts at potential employers, serve as references during a job search, or may even become a laid-off person's next employer."

And remember, even as an organization seems mired in trouble, team leaders can turn lemons into lemonade by channeling energy into tangible accomplishments.

In the summer of 2008, even though Lehman Brothers was clearly heading south, Anne Erni, then chief diversity officer, pulled her team members together, identified three priorities on their annual to-do list, and insisted they accomplish those specific goals.

"I didn't care if management never looked at what we did," she says. "Even when it looked as though the game was over, I told my team to keep playing. I told them to keep hitting the flippers and maybe the ball would pop out." By focusing her staff on concrete, doable tasks, Erni not only produced potentially valuable programs for the organization (for example, a plan to "leverage inclusion" after Barclays and Lehman merged) but also distracted her people from panic. And because Erni's team engaged in tasks that also benefited them as individual professionals, when the ax fell, they entered the job market with impressive resumes and recent accomplishments to their credit.

Create Career Opportunities

A players have high expectations for their career trajectories; they want to excel, not only remain employed. But as budgets shrink, formal professional development courses are often cut—at a time when people want to enhance and burnish their skills to remain marketable. Team leaders can pick up the slack here. With raises off the table and promotions rare, one of the most valuable things a manager can do is make a visible commitment to a high-potential employee's career.

Ironically, tough times offer plenty of scope for career development. When teams are operating with skeleton staffs everyone must pitch in, and a thoughtful team leader can use straitened circumstances to help strong performers gain access to stretch assignments or cross functional roles—opportunities that normally would not be available to them.

In fall 2008, in the midst of massive layoffs and defections, Dana (a fictitious name), a first-year associate at a large bank in New York, was given a large regional transaction to work on because the person who structured and sold the transaction had been let go. It was a huge opportunity, and Dana leapt at it although it meant committing to fourteen-hour days.

It's been a heady experience. In her words, "I'm running a transaction that's a big portion of my unit's revenue stream. Effectively, as a first-year associate, I'm doing the job of a vice president. I've learned a ton, and the transaction's gone well. I now know that I can do this on my own without much guidance."

This stretch assignment, however, has come with a downside: Dana has been largely ignored by her team leader. That neglect is eating into her motivation.

A smart manager would use this constellation of events to motivate Dana, recognizing and celebrating her efforts to go above and beyond. Best of all would be to bring her performance to the attention of higher-ups so that this stretch assignment could potentially accelerate her career. None of this has happened for Dana. Her manager is distracted and tuned out, and Dana is beginning to see her energy flag. "You say to yourself, 'Wow, I'm taking on a lot more responsibility; I'm working really hard—staying until eleven at night. I'm not getting compensated, I'm not getting recognized. Why should I pull all the stops out if there's nothing in it for me?'"

In addition to stretch assignments (properly managed), you can build engagement by encouraging your high-potential employees to expand their professional network of colleagues, internal customers, or suppliers. Target cross-functional projects that leverage your employee's skill set and also introduce the opportunity to grow and learn in a new market. Share the big picture so that team members have a better understanding of the significance of what they do, and include them in the decision-making process so that they feel their voice is being heard.

Another option: let your *A* team loose on tough problems the organization is trying to crack. Prepare to be surprised: if you ask the right people the right questions, then a week or so later they may come back and say, "I've been turning this over in my mind, and I've got something to share with you." It may not be a complete solution, but it could be an idea that leads to a breakthrough. Giving people a sense that they have contributed to the solution of an important problem drives ownership at a grassroots level and makes everyone feel good.

Encourage Active Mentoring

At Alcoa, Judith Nocito has started recent staff meetings spotlighting one person for something significant she has recently worked on, sharing the accomplishment with the rest of the team. It can be as mundane as e-mailing a client a well-crafted analysis of an issue, or as significant as the resolution of a complex trade compliance issue. "People appreciate the opportunity to shine in front of their peers," Nocito says. And by leveraging teachable moments, this practice helps everyone become better at her job.

Not every boss has the array of skills required to effectively mentor and manage the careers of high-potential young employees. But getting partway there can be powerful. This is because career barriers are particularly distressing for top talent. Even in tough times, *A* players easily disengage if they feel their company is not maximizing their development.

Two years ago an internal survey at professional services firm KPMG revealed that many of its high-potential employees wanted to enhance their relationship with their performance managers. In response, the firm identified a team of proven mentors to give the most valuable employees—client-facing associates—more robust career guidance. These *people management leaders* (PMLs) are responsible for all areas of an associate's work experience—from work–life balance issues to an optimal mix of client assignments to career progression challenges.

After a one-year pilot, employees who had been assigned a PML reported a 10 to 15 percent gain in satisfaction with career opportunities at the firm. KPMG expanded the initiative, and by early 2009 it had identified twenty-six hundred PMLs to mentor seventeen thousand client-service employees; the program now involves 70 percent of the workforce. Although this expansion was not a reaction to the recession, Bruce Pfau, KPMG's vice chair of human resources, reports that the program is "serving the firm particularly well in this economic downturn, enhancing employee engagement when times are tough."

3: Give Employees Meaningful Nonmonetary Rewards

Reality bites hard these days. "Last year I was managing 70 people, all located in New York," reported one participant in a Hidden Brain Drain strategy session. "This year, after layoffs, I manage 125 people in New York, London, Paris, Hong Kong, and Tokyo. The number of managers has been reduced, and I've had to take on additional groups around the world. Hours are crazy because of the global scope of my new responsibilities."

With salaries dwindling and the scope of work on the rise, managers can no longer rely on financial incentives to keep their A players performing at their peak. Instead, managers are forced to find new and creative ways of motivating top performers to give their best. From a simple but heartfelt "Thank you" to acknowledge dedication and hard work, to inventive ways of positioning time as currency, there's a rich menu of alternatives to monetary rewards.

Don't Forget to Say, "Thank You"

"Never in the field of human conflict was so much owed by so many to so few." With that immortal phrase of appreciation, Winston Churchill ensured that no one would forget the efforts of the Royal Air Force in beating back the Luftwaffe in the Battle of Britain.

Matching Churchill's eloquence is a daunting goal, but figuring out how to simply acknowledge hard work and heroic effort is a huge step in the right direction. Data from Hidden Brain Drain strategy sessions repeatedly underscores this principle. In the words of one participant, "Thanking people for their hard work and commitment is the key to making them feel appreciated."

"Because few people expect much in the way of reward these days, a small but personalized 'Thank you' can have a big impact," says Steve Richardson of American Express. "I try to personalize everything. Even when I send a recognition note to a big group or team, I try to add a personalized paragraph in each person's e-mail so it's highly tailored to the individual."

Public recognition is also a powerful tool; it doesn't cost money but can reap a huge return. For example, Cisco uses its Collaboration Across Cisco award to recognize employees who have had exceptional success using Web 2.0 technology to collaborate with other employees, customers, or partners. Every few months a winning team is showcased at the company's quarterly meeting, and its successful projects (along with those of four finalists) are shared on the company's intranet. At year end an overall winning team is selected, and a $5,000 charitable contribution is made in the team's name.

A senior executive spending personal time with an employee is another popular reward. "Being taken to lunch or breakfast by the boss once in a while not only shows appreciation but interest," says one strategy session participant.

"Just be sure not to devalue your appreciation with overenthusiasm," warns another participant. "Thank-yous are only appreciated if they are heartfelt and not just token." And even though it's understood that stressful times make people snappish, sprinkling around a few "good jobs" doesn't make up for bad behavior. "It's extremely important to treat people nicely in times like these," the participant added.

Promote Existing Wellness Benefits

Study after study shows that high levels of stress, experienced day in and day out, are significantly detrimental to health and well-being. Scientists warn that stress contributes to health problems ranging from obesity and diabetes to heart disease and infertility. One study shows that working more than sixty hours a week and failing to get regular sleep can double the risk of having a heart attack. But only 28 percent of Americans say that they do a good job of managing stress.

Companies need to get involved. Not only does stress undermine the health of employees—reducing resilience and undermining performance—but also it can directly impact the bottom line. Merrill Lynch found that health care costs at the company shot up in 2008, a year of great turmoil, as many employees leaned heavily on medical services. Stress, it turns out, costs money.

Organizations can help employees build resilience and keep in peak form by reminding them about company-sponsored (and outside) initiatives that offer aids to physical wellness—stress management, smoke-cessation programs, cancer screening, and the like. In recent months, Goldman Sachs and Pfizer—among others—have reached out to the Maurer Foundation for Breast Health Education to present programs that demystify breast cancer and champion early detection through mammography, clinical breast examination, and monthly self-examination. Overloaded executives welcome these reminders—in the midst of a global recession it's so easy to neglect oneself. One female manager described the Maurer Foundation program as a "wake-up call"—it spurred her to perform a self-examination that led to the discovery of a small lump—and early-on treatable cancer.

Many companies already offer on-site gyms or free memberships to local health clubs. But even though periodic memos might encourage employees to take advantage of these facilities, stressed-out participants in Hidden Brain Drain strategy sessions say that's not enough: "In this environment it's easy to feel guilty about taking time out to go to the gym," said one participant. "It attracts negative attention. Colleagues question whether you've gotten your priorities straight."

If you want to show your employees that you really care about them, one of the strongest signals you can send is making it easy for them to exercise. But how do you position or justify this in a recession when everyone needs to be on the case all the time? One manager solved this problem by creating a workout rotation for his team: each person signed up for a different time slot, ensuring that the team was never seriously depleted.

At Ernst & Young, partners have access to a variety of wellness and leadership programs which can be customized based on their needs. These programs include day-long health physicals at renowned health and wellness facilities, training on energy management and wellness, and whole-life coaching. One whole-life coaching program covers physical fitness, family dynamics, financial health, and career development over a 12-month period. "The hope of the program is that people who have become depleted will be rejuvenated," says Carolyn Buck Luce, who went through the program. "The symbolism is powerful. For the firm to let you know that they want to invest in you—in the full round of your life—sends a tremendous message. And because the coaching is tailored to the specifics of the E&Y culture and customized to fit the needs of men, women, and multicultural executives, it helps our top talent maintain their enthusiasm and energy throughout the various stages of their careers."

Use Time as Currency

Tough times are the right time to formalize flexible work schedules. Companies that treat time as currency—through remote work options, staggered hours, reduced-hour arrangements, and mini-sabbaticals—earn the appreciation and loyalty of their high performers. Such employers also drive performance;

by offering a rich menu of flexible work arrangements, they are more likely to attract and retain talented employees than companies that do not. "Flexibility is one of the most important aspects of being a competitive employer," says Kerrie Peraino, chief diversity officer at American Express.

Flexibility is a powerful lure in recruiting high-caliber people. Work–life balance has always been prized by working women juggling the demands of family and high-powered jobs, and now these moms are being seconded by members of the incoming Generation Y cohort, who consider it a basic entitlement to play as hard as they work.

When companies allow people to work from home for part of one or two days a week, they gain numerous low-cost, high-return advantages. The most obvious payoff: employees are able to concentrate without being interrupted by phone calls, meetings, and other workplace distractions. Eliminating watercooler gossip sessions—a significant time sink in a high-anxiety environment—is a huge boost to productivity. In the words of one strategy session participant, "People are much more productive when they can avoid office chitchat and eliminate useless commuting time. A day to focus without constant interruption can be really valuable." And when comp is down, the cost savings associated with flexibility are important. "Savings on commuting costs can be huge!" added another participant.

In April 2009, the U.S.-based office of Booz & Company replaced its longtime unpaid sabbatical policy with a new Partial-Pay Sabbatical program. The new program, available to *all* employees—not just consultants—offers participants between one to twelve months off, during which employees receive 20 percent of their base salary, full health-care benefits, and a guarantee that, when they return, they will have their job for at least as many months they took time away from the company. First offered in Europe in early 2009, where uptake has been over 30 percent, Partial-Pay Sabbatical is much more than a cost-management tool—the global consulting firm sees it as a way to increase engagement by allowing people to relax, advance their education, spend time with family, volunteer for a charitable organization, or even take on a part-time job to gain additional experience.

Flexible work arrangements can also potentially benefit employers by bringing down the fixed costs of office real estate. The proverbial lightbulb went on in Citigroup's corporate real estate division when it was discovered that too many real lightbulbs were shining in too many empty offices. On any given day, the occupancy rate of Citi's offices was at best 60 percent. The company was wasting resources on offices that no one was using. The result: Citigroup's Alternative Workplace Strategy, or AWS, program. In addition to driving cost savings through remote working, use of hotels, and moving of people to less-expensive offices, AWS is a key element in Citigroup's newly positioned and newly enhanced flexible work strategy, itself a strong recruitment and retention tool for Gen Y and female employees.

AWS will launch globally in mid-2009. By 2011, Citi hopes that most employees will have moved into one of the many "space solutions" offered through the AWS program. The goal is to shave 15 percent off the company's global office space needs, which will have significant cost savings over a three-year period. Citi expects the AWS program to also help drive down attrition rates, because of the greater flexibility offered to employees. This will produce additional cost savings for the company.

Paradoxically, although an increasing number of organizations have come to realize that all hands can still be on deck even if not all bodies are at their desks, tough times deter employees from taking advantage of flexible hours. Even those who would benefit most from working at home feel they dare not do it. "Sadly, there's a stigma, which seems to have gotten worse in this recession," notes one strategy session participant. Explains another, "Working remotely from home looks less 'dedicated,' even though most people work even harder at home and, interestingly, are more often available."

One solution is to position flexibility as a business imperative. Historically, Sodexo, a leading provider of food and facilities management solutions, worked with employees to create flexible schedules on a case-by-case basis. But in 2008 the company launched a formal flexible work arrangement that is business based. Flexibility must be mutually beneficial, for both the business as well as for the employee. Rather than managers deciding on an ad hoc basis which employees would be allowed to telecommute or flex their schedules, managers now follow corporate procedures and evaluate flexible work proposals against business needs and impact.

Flexibility is no longer a favor or perceived as an entitlement. To qualify, employees must be in good standing and have no past or current performance issues. Eligible employees complete their own flexible arrangement proposals, and managers assess whether the arrangements will allow workers to meet performance and productivity goals. Each flexible arrangement begins with a trial period, with biannual reviews to gauge success and fix problems. Employees must resubmit a flex request each year, so renewal is not automatic but earned.

For top talent, flexibility is an important aspirational goal. Even if they cannot avail themselves of flexible hours right now, hard-driving high performers who routinely give 110 percent to the job can dream about how things can change as soon as the load lightens. Companies that want to keep their best people would be wise to heed this comment from a strategy session participant: "I'm the primary breadwinner, so I can't take time off now. But in looking for a new job, a role with flexibility will be my top choice."

Encourage Employees to Do Good on Company Time

As you will see in section 7, corporate social responsibility (CSR) or social outreach activities are a proven win-win situation for organizations and their employees. One way companies can reward top talent is to make it easier for employees to volunteer on company time. BT recently tweaked its corporate social responsibility (CSR) initiative. According to a recent internal survey, more than one third of UK telecommunications giant BT's employees are already active volunteers on their own time and another 30 percent would like to volunteer but are not yet doing so. In April 2009, BT established a first-ever coordinated, companywide volunteer program, realizing that this could be a key factor in motivating and retaining high-potential employees. The new program will make it easier for BT's 106,000 employees to volunteer their time and expertise. "We are looking at ways in which volunteering can make a strategic difference to our business, and develop activities and partners around that," says Helen Simpson who is leading BT's new program. "The skills people develop while volunteering are central to many of our operations, so we can use volunteering to develop our talent pool and accelerate learning."

Tough economic times impact the performance of the most important people in an organization. Companies need to understand that they can no longer motivate top talent in the traditional way—through enhanced compensation—and need to look instead for imaginative ways to boost performance, thereby building a strong foundation for growth and renewal.

4: Develop a Fair Restructuring Process

"The layoffs happened on the sixteenth," recalls Tom (a fictitious name), a survivor of a massive bloodletting at a large financial services firm. He continues,

> They occurred in a glass-walled conference room at the back of the trading floor. It was a like a goldfish bowl—so exposed. And to make matters worse, when people left the conference room with a blue folder with the severance information tucked under their arm, they had to walk all the way across the trading floor—hundreds of feet—where they knew a lot of people, and everyone could see that you had that telltale folder and would understand that the person had been fired. It was like running the gauntlet. Everyone was treated this way, associates all the way up to managing directors. The building was abuzz. Employees on other floors found out—via phone and e-mail—who had

gotten laid off before the names were officially announced, because the traders on the floor spread the word. People in other banks also knew, because traders talk to each other all the time. What they were saying was, "I can't believe that's how they're laying people off! That company is a mess. They don't know what they're doing."

From the vantage point of Tom, a high-performing young associate, "that decision—to conduct layoffs in such a conspicuous and humiliating way—cost the firm a great deal of loyalty and respect, not just within the organization but all across Wall Street."

Reductions in force (RIFs) have become a grim reality, but bad downsizing can be bad for morale and bad for business. Participants in Hidden Brain Drain strategy sessions were honest when assessing the impact of layoffs on their state of mind: some 73 percent talked about being demoralized, 64 percent talked about being demotivated, and 74 percent talked about shutting down and turning off.

"Terms of disengagement" matter. Poorly handled RIFs leave a bad taste in the mouths of those employees shown the door *and* those picked to stay. Wayne Cascio, a business school professor at the University of Colorado at Denver, looked at eighteen years' worth of downsizing data and found that even though expenses drop in the wake of large layoffs, revenues tend to drop, too—often disproportionately. This is because the remaining workers are coping with *survivor syndrome*—the anger, fear, anxiety, and decreased risk taking that follow a mass firing. Just when a company needs employees to charge over the hill to turn the organization around, they retreat to the bunkers.

These losses have the potential to multiply. The talented employees you toss on the scrap heap will be back in the marketplace—as customers, clients, and, when business picks up, competitors, eager to lure your top performers to their teams. And if those top performers are still scarred by a callous layoff, they won't think twice about leaving.

In short, managers need to pay close attention to their remaining star performers during a restructuring. If RIFs are unavoidable, how do you protect and reassure your stars? How can you hold on to their best energies even as you let their colleagues go?

Start by reminding yourself that smart people aren't stupid, and commit to being a straight shooter.

Commit to Transparency

Managers confronting painful RIFs usually want to get the bad stuff over with as quickly as possible and get back to work. No one wants to deal with the emotions of a wounded colleague. Yet that's exactly what is necessary to prevent festering of anger and resentment and to reassure your remaining people that they are still safe.

"You can't tell people they are walking the plank without telling them why," says Tom Stewart of Booz & Company. "Help people understand *why* you jettisoned the buggy-whip division."

As you explain the reasons for these difficult decisions, describe the train of thought that led to this outcome. Ideally, managers want their ex-employees to look back and say, "Yes, I understand why I was let go," even if they are still angry.

Reflexite, a Connecticut-based company that manufactures products for fire departments around the country, recently developed a business decline contingency plan that identifies four stages of decline and points to steps that should be taken to cope with each stage as it emerges. Layoffs can happen only at stage 4, after all kinds of avoidance action has been taken by management as well as workers.

The benefit of this kind of contingency plan is the security it gives employees of knowing that many efforts will be made before the company gets to the point of letting people go. And managers are secure, knowing that employees are devoting their best energy to turning the company around and in the end will support the company's action.

Not only the plan but also the process must be fair. That means allowing people—those who leave and those who stay—to *see* the process. One way to think about this: do not do anything behind closed doors that you would not want to read about online.

When an L.A.-based advertising company was forced to lay off employees early in 2009, the company created a process designed to be as humane as possible, both for those let go and those who stayed. Because their offices have an open layout and conference rooms have glass walls, people being given the bad news were asked to go to a different floor in the building, that was not being used—a traditional office suite with solid walls—that offered privacy.

In many RIFs, laid-off workers are immediately escorted off the premises by security guards. "We tried to design different options so as to make the process as comfortable as possible," said the head of human resources for the company. Rather than being marched through a lockstep process, people were given choices: they could pack up their desks, or they could have the firm pack their belongings; they could take their boxes with them, or they could have the firm ship them; they could say good-bye to their colleagues, or they could decide to leave immediately.

This unconventional approach might be seen as risky, but the firm decided it was a risk they were willing to take. It had real payoffs for the employees involved. The HR head gave an example: "In one case, a group of people who had been let go held a vigil in an area of the building where they knew colleagues would see them." "The vigil morphed into an impromptu gathering which was part support group and part good-bye party. While sad, this gathering gave departing employees a measure of dignity—and comfort—and left those who were staying with a sense of closure."

Make Layoffs Easier on Managers

The heaviest burden in a restructuring is often borne by line managers, who must translate the impersonal order "reduce head count by 20 percent" into brutal encounters with real people. Not only are the actual conversations daunting, but also they leave behind residual guilt, ill will, and sadness. Yes, a manager will be relieved that her own job is intact, but it is painful to put people on the street, especially in a down cycle, when the prospect of quickly finding a new position is dim.

Many of these line managers may, in fact, be the stars you most need to keep. Stuck in the cross fire, they need sympathy and support.

If you supervise a manager who must execute layoffs, pay attention to that manager's potential stress and strain. Be aware that he may be hesitant to acknowledge anxieties either to himself or to colleagues. Support can include role-playing the actual dismissal conversation or helping him decide whom to let go. Simply acknowledging the difficulty of the situation can help mitigate the emotional tax on managers who must deliver the bad news.

One way to lighten the load on managers is to reduce the number of redundancies by a creative use of flexible work arrangements.

The economic downturn has hit professional services firms hard. U.K. accounting giant KPMG has developed an imaginative contingency plan called Flexible Futures, which was designed to decrease payroll costs while at the same time maintain the firm's deep commitment to its people.

In January 2009, the firm gave its eleven thousand U.K.-based employees a four-way choice. They could volunteer for a four-day workweek and a 20 percent reduction in base pay; they could opt for a four- to twelve-week sabbatical at 30 percent base pay; they could opt for both; or they could stick to their current deal. Once staff volunteer, the decision to implement rests solely with the firm, although consideration is given to personal preferences.

Positioned as a way for the firm to "come together" in tough times, Flexible Futures is already seen as a winner. "We were trying to deal with reality but also give employees some control over their own destiny," says Rachel Campbell, head of people for KPMG Europe and architect of Flexible Futures. To date 85 percent of KPMG's U.K.-based employees have signed up for a flexible future, opting for one of the first three choices. The most popular choice is option 3, which features both a shorter workweek and a sabbatical. This choice gives a sense of how time-starved professionals are. According to Campbell, "Given this, the company is looking at an immediate savings opportunity of 15 percent of payroll costs."

Although Flexible Futures is driven by cost savings pressure, Campbell is convinced that the plan will boost morale in a company that is already rich in esprit de corps. KPMG was recently named "top company to work for" by London's *Sunday Times*.

Help Employees Help Themselves

One of the reasons RIFs continue to resonate among survivors is that even prized performers feel their future is uncertain. Realistically, there's no way for employers to guarantee that more layoffs won't happen. You can, however, reassure your top players by helping your critical core team members strengthen their safety nets.

In early 2008, the International Monetary Fund (IMF) downsized its workforce for the first time since its founding in 1944, a traumatic event for this usually stable organization of twenty-six hundred employees. To bolster morale, Dominique Strauss-Kahn, managing director, personally reached out to sister organizations such as the United Nations and the World Bank, to inquire about job openings and to request that IMF-ers be treated as "internal staff" and given preference when applying for jobs.

Helping displaced employees network and scope out what might be a next job—in other divisions or other organizations—reaffirms their value and minimizes ill will. At the same time, it lets the remaining employees know that management cares enough to do more than just wish them good luck. Going the extra mile builds a kind of loyalty that won't be forgotten.

Booz & Company—in the manner of many top-notch consulting firms—makes cuts every year, asking about 15 percent of its professional labor force to move on to another career. This is known as the "up or on" career model in management consulting. Rather than just letting them go—wishing them good luck and providing a standard severance package—partners and senior staff at Booz reach out to help find the next job, tapping in to a network of former Booz consultants and clients. According to DeAnne Aguirre, SVP and senior partner, "Using the power of the company to help find the next job makes people who are being let go feel better, and allows 'survivors'—employees who make the cut and stay with the company—to assuage their guilt and feel that they did what they could to help."

In this time of deep recession, companies are beginning to recognize the value of creating a talent bank of employees who need to take time off—understanding that they may want to tap in to this valuable pool when conditions improve.

Don't Just Cut—Create!

There's got to be a morning after
If we can hold on through the night
We have a chance to find the sunshine
Let's keep on looking for the light.

No one my age can forget this song from *The Poseidon Adventure*, a movie about a supposedly unsinkable ship being flipped over and sunk by a rogue wave. But just as a lucky few survive in the story, so organizations can emerge from tough times stronger and more resilient. The key is to restructure in a way that is both responsible and responsive to new opportunities.

At Time Warner, Lisa Quiroz's answer to budget cuts was not simply to maintain a smaller version of the status quo. She held an off-site meeting for her staff and told them to get creative. "Rather than trim what we did, I challenged my staff to rethink the whole thing. I told them, 'Make believe we were starting from zero. If you were told you had X amount of money and had to build a program, what would it look like?' I wanted them to focus on opportunity, not loss. So we did some jiggering. Psychologically, it helped."

For leaders who see their people as assets to be developed rather than costs to be cut, restructuring offers an opportunity to change the way leaders operate to make better use of the talent they have. And by being seen to make smart new choices in difficult times, they can spark a kind of creativity and commitment that money can't buy.

5: Hold On to Your Women

We've seen the headlines. In March 2009 *Forbes* ran a cover story that featured a picture of five knock-your-socks-off, newly fired female bankers—all rising stars—along with a headline that screamed, "Wall Street's Disappearing Women." In the worst financial crash since the Depression, financial services and insurance firms have cut 126,000 jobs. Of these laid-off workers, 72 percent have been women, even though they constituted a smaller proportion (64 percent) of total employment in the sector before the crash began.

Hard figures are beginning to come in confirming two kinds of attrition among women in this recession: women are being disproportionately let go, particularly in certain key sectors. They are also disproportionately quitting—voluntarily leaving their jobs. Data from Hidden Brain Drain strategy sessions shows that women were more than twice as likely as men (84 percent compared with 40 percent) to have one foot out the door.

Whether forced or voluntary, a female exodus is bad for business. Losing any top talent is expensive for an organization; losing high-performing female talent is expensive in the short term and has serious long-term ramifications.

Links to the Bottom Line

Having significant numbers of women in management positions improves a company's bottom line. Research conducted by both Catalyst and McKinsey & Company demonstrates that companies that do well by women have a much higher return on investment (ROI) than companies that do poorly. Women have the smarts, outperforming men in tertiary education systems around the world. They also have the power of the purse. According to management guru Tom Peters, women make 83 percent of all purchases. Companies trying to design and market winning products in a tight global market need to have a lot of tuned-in women on their teams—including leading those teams—or else they will find themselves outcompeted. The conventional adage that "the customer is king" is actually dead wrong. The customer isn't king: she's queen.

In addition, a new study from London Business School shows that when work teams boast a 50-50 split in men and women, productivity goes up. This research argues that gender balance counters *groupthink*—the tendency of homogenous groups to staunchly defend wrongheaded ideas because everyone in the group thinks the same way.

There's even compelling new evidence that the global financial crisis might have been mitigated had there been less testosterone in top management. "Global Financial Crisis: Are Women the Antidote?" a study published in October 2008 by CERAM Business School, shows that firms in the CAC40 (the French equivalent of the Dow Jones Industrial Average) with a high ratio of women in top management have shown better resistance to the financial crisis. The fewer female managers a company has, the greater the drop in its share price since January 2008. For example, BNP Paribas, where 39 percent of managers are women, has seen its stock price fall by 20 percent since the beginning of 2008; Credit Agricole, on the other hand, where only 16 percent of managers are female, saw its share price drop by 50 percent. Michel Ferrary, the report's author, concludes, "The feminization of management seems to be a protection against financial crisis."

Not "Men in Skirts"

The first step for companies wanting to hold on to—and make the most of—their high-performing women is to understand why they might want to leave. It's not that smart women aren't deeply committed to their careers or that they don't need to work. Our data shows that in December 2008, despite industry smackdowns, fewer than a quarter (22 percent) of high-performing women who had "one foot out the door" planned to take time out of the workforce. Most were seeking less onerous—and more meaningful—work.

At the heart of the problem is the fact that women are not male clones—not merely "men in skirts," as the saying goes. Research by ISR (International Survey Research) reveals that equally talented men and women march to different drummers. According to this study, the top two drivers for male executives are career advancement and financial rewards, whereas the top two drivers for their female counterparts are high-quality colleagues and the desire to deliver a quality product to a customer or client.

Data from a recent Hidden Brain Drain study lays out a complex vision of what high-powered women really want. At the top of the wish list is a series of career goals that speak to the quality of the work experience itself. Talented women very much want to associate with people they respect (82 percent); to "be themselves" at work (79 percent); to collaborate with others and work as part of a team (61 percent); and to give back to society through the work they do (56 percent).[5] They also value recognition from their company or organization (51 percent). Access to flexible work schedules, the only employment benefit on the female wish list, is a priority for 64 percent. Financial rewards are less important: only 42 percent of women cite a high salary as an important career goal.

Because their ambitions are constructed and fueled in ways far more multidimensional than making money, women are always revisiting priorities and recalibrating at the margin. As described in part 1 of this book, women are constantly asking the question, Are the opportunity costs associated with holding a high-pressure job—the missed family dinners, the working vacations—worth the benefits?

For many women involved in this constant recalibration, a nudge or a push—the departure of an admired boss, work demands spiraling up—is all it takes to shift the cost calculation in the wrong direction. Wrong, that is, for the employer.

What Companies Can Do

Over the past several years we've made progress on the retention and acceleration of women. Indeed, in the 2004–2008 period I spurred action among the companies that make up the Hidden Brain Drain task force. Over five years we've developed a core agenda and seeded seventy models of best practice that helped companies get up and running.

What is this action plan? For a detailed agenda see my book *Off-Ramps and On-Ramps* (Boston: Harvard Business School Press, 2007). Following are three basics.

1. Establish a Rich Menu of Flexible Work Arrangements

Flexible work arrangements go to the heart of what women want most. They dominate women's wish lists. Reduced-hour options, flexible stop and start times, telecommuting, job sharing, and seasonal flexibility—time off in the summer, balanced by longer hours in the winter—are among the programs women yearn for. Many high performers see flexible work arrangements as a lifesaver, eliminating the need to quit a hard-won, much-valued job.

Flexible work arrangements are becoming more important in this recession. With pressure ramping up, increasing numbers of talented women want and need to flex their schedules.

2. Help Women Claim and Sustain Ambition

The data shows a serious falloff in ambition as women move through their thirties. Confounded by the escalating pressures of outsize jobs and penalized for taking a brief off-ramp, many talented women downsize their expectations. This is a huge issue. An employer cannot promote a woman if she herself is not greatly vested in this endeavor.

Women's networks are part of the solution. At the simplest level, they boost confidence by connecting women to their peers. Often, high-performing women feel isolated—marooned in a sea of men. In addition, networks provide access to senior women who can act as mentors and role models; serve as a showcase for presentation and organizational skills; and expand business relationships—both within the company and on the outside.

3. Harness Altruism

As you have learned, the aspirations of talented women are multidimensional and tend not to be dominated by money. Financial compensation is important to women, but it's not nearly as important as meaning and purpose. In Hidden Brain Drain strategy sessions women talked eloquently about their commitment to giving back to their communities (both their corporate community and those on the outside). Whether it's saving the wetlands or feeding the homeless, talented women want to help heal the planet and improve the lot of humankind.

These and other action items developed by the leading-edge corporations that make up the Hidden Brain Drain Task Force have helped drive significant change.

For example, GE has moved the dial on senior women. Partly because of the efforts of its enormously effective Women's Network program, 16 percent of GE's top corporate officers are now women, up from 12 percent a few years ago. Johnson & Johnson has also created a powerful women's network—the Women's Leadership Initiative, or WLI—which has accelerated progress, transforming the numbers of women in top ranks. Some 30 percent of vice president positions are now held by women, and the J&J board of directors is 20 percent female. And Ernst & Young has made impressive strides. Today, all employees are given the opportunity to work flexibly and 10 percent of partners work on formal flexible work arrangements, as do approximately 30 percent of those on the rung just below partner. By creating a flexible and reduced-hour career track that takes you all the way to the top, E&Y has been able to hold on to a large number of its high-performing women.

The Impact of the Recession

The action agenda described here has been affected by the brutal economic downturn. Some standout players (think Lehman Brothers) have disappeared, and even GE, Johnson & Johnson, and Ernst & Young have had to prune programs and cut costs. But it would be wrong to assume that action has stopped— that CEOs have somehow forgotten that there's a compelling business case to hold on to high-performing women. Indeed, some of the more prescient are discovering that now might be an excellent time to ramp up the women's agenda.

On March 19, 2009, in Munich, German engineering giant Siemens launched its very first Diversity Day during which they unveiled GLOW, a new global network geared to the needs of the company's talented women. The launch, presided over by CEO Peter Loescher, marked the first step in the rollout of an ambitious program that seeks to accelerate female progress particularly at the top of the house. This is an unprecedented step for an industrial juggernaut where the CEO, in November 2008, made a bold visionary step to appoint an Asian woman as the first chief diversity officer in Siemens' 162 years. Currently only 7 percent of senior management is female.

When asked why Siemens was launching a ground-breaking women's leadership initiative in a year when most companies were hunkering down, Loescher talked about links to performance and innovation and stressed that female talent was "the biggest untapped lever" in driving the company's bottom line. He also talked about the "opportunities for leapfrogging in this crisis. Precisely because we're doing better than other industrial players, this is an excellent time for us to surge ahead of competitors and attract and engage highly qualified women around the world."

But you don't have to be a new player to see the urgency of the women's agenda in this recession. Citi is repositioning and expanding its flexibility programs, and Intel is newly emphasizing programs that target technical women.

"For us, brain share is critical in up and down economies," says Rosalind Hudnell, corporate director of diversity at Intel. "We're just focused on retaining key talent in these tough times." To ensure that it hangs on to its women, Intel has created two projects that provide traction for female engineers: the Technical Female Leadership Series and the Women Principal Engineers' Forum. Both of these programs help women hone their readiness for principal engineering positions. The Forum program has been particularly successful. Designed for women and led by women Fellows and principal engineers, it has been credited directly with doubling the number of women Fellows and nearly doubling Intel's female principal engineer population over the past few years.

UBS, to its great credit given the problems that have beset the financial services industry over the last eighteen months, recently piloted two new programs aimed at supporting female officers. Connecting with Clients in Turbulent Times is an initiative designed to increase engagement, productivity, and profitability for some of the bank's client-facing female officers; this three-month program is tailored to women who want to take their revenue generation skills to the next level. Charting Your Future is a career counseling workshop customized for high-powered women in Asia. "Participants list their priorities—in both their personal and their work lives—and then work with a team to figure out how they can achieve these priorities so that there's no second-guessing about choices and goals," explains Mona Lau, global head of diversity and campus recruiting at UBS. "The message from management is that the bank cares, we want you to stay and will respect your personal choices."

Protect Your Brand

Failure to hold on to women—particularly senior women in this recession—creates two kinds of problems over the long run.

First, companies deplete their pipeline. When women at the top of the house are disproportionately fired—or disproportionately quit—it starts a downward spiral that's difficult to break. Once you lose a cohort of senior female leaders, you lose the sponsors, mentors, and role models needed to inspire the generation of young women coming up through the ranks. And you tear a hole in the network for future female recruits. In short you risk emptying your pool of female talent into the distant future.

Second, companies risk tarnishing their reputation and brand. "Appearances are often more important than facts," says Anne Erni. During Lehman's three rounds of layoffs before the firm went bankrupt, there was a widespread perception among its women that female employees were being affected more than men. Erni oversaw an analysis that found that women typically were not impacted in greater numbers. But, she adds, "Psychologically, if you lose two out of ten women and twenty out of one hundred men, those two women are worth a hell of a lot more."

The lesson here is to protect your good name in this recession. Understand that a carefully tended track record as an employer of choice for women can be undermined in a nanosecond. It's easy to damage a reputation, and companies can't afford to risk access to high-octane female brainpower.

6: Show That Top Leadership Cares

CEOs play an extraordinarily powerful role in shaping attitudes and behavior within an organization. Through what they say, the tone of what they say, and where they say it, they can shift corporate culture. Their message cascades down through all layers of leadership and connects with employees at all levels in the company.

Thus, CEOs—and the occupants of the C-suite—need to get heavily involved in the struggle to energize top talent. Now's the time to show your high performers—your stars—that top leadership cares. Shout this message from the rooftops. Whether it's front-loaded in an interview for *Wall Street Week* or featured in a high-profile blog on the company's intranet, a smart CEO's stump speech tells the world, "Our people are our greatest asset in these troubled times," and smart CEOs then follow through with concrete actions.

To be sure, recessionary times compress a leader's calendar even more than usual. It's tempting to think that your time is more valuably spent hashing out a survival strategy than giving pep talks. But the contrary is true. Company survival is more likely to depend on your ability to turbocharge the brainpower that will drive renewal and growth.

What are some of the most effective—and efficient—ways to show that you care?

Increase Touch Points

Film director Woody Allen famously said that 80 percent of success is just showing up. It's difficult to stress enough the significance of forging a personal connection with your key people, especially in these times of uncertainty. When no one's job is safe—and your top talent is too savvy to fall for cookie-cutter corporate assurances—just knowing that they're not alone in a Darwinian fight for survival is a lifeline.

As mentioned before, Webcasts, e-mail blasts, teleconferences, virtual town hall meetings—all these cyberspace tools serve valuable communication functions. But none should replace the reassurance of actual person-to-person connection and interaction.

In 2008, facing a tough economic environment and fundamental changes in the media industry, Time Warner took steps to strengthen its competitive advantages by becoming a more focused content company. The company's restructuring, including the spinoff of Time Warner Cable in early 2008, has involved streamlining its operations and reducing overhead to make its businesses as efficient as possible and free up resources. This has been a difficult process for employees across the company.

As part of an effort to engage high-potential employees, many of whom felt embattled, the company's newly appointed CEO, Jeffrey L. Bewkes, held a series of six skip-level lunches, reaching beyond his direct reports and inviting groups of ten to twelve high performers several layers down in the organization—people who usually had little or no access to him. These employees were considered to be connectors and influencers and would likely share their luncheon experience—and the CEO's words—with colleagues. In this way, a gathering for a few could have far-reaching impact.

These two-hour lunches were unscripted. The point was to have an open conversation that allowed Bewkes to take the pulse of the organization's emerging leaders and permitted these highly valued individuals to get to know their new CEO.

The feedback from both sides underscored the importance of these lunches. Employees who attended reported feeling more "confident in the company" and described the CEO as being "open," "approachable," even "funny." For his part, "the CEO was impressed by how much people cared about the company," says Patricia Fili-Krushel, Time Warner's executive vice president of administration, who organized the meetings. The lunches proved to be such a valuable use of the chief executive's time that the company is continuing them in their divisions in 2009.

Skip-level lunches are an especially valuable engagement tool because they can be adapted to many circumstances. For example, in the face of clampdowns on travel, companies are leveraging their leaders' travel itineraries to create touch points for key talent around the world.

Lynn Utter of Knoll insisted on preserving two core corporate events in 2008 despite their associated expenses. First, she refused to cancel Knoll's annual leadership conference, where one hundred of its most senior managers convene. Second, Knoll not only held its midyear sales conference but also doubled attendance to include all of its three hundred salespeople.

"Knoll kept travel costs in check by opting for less costly venues than in the past," says Utter. But the money and time spent were well worth it. For Utter, the meetings were an unparalleled opportunity for the company's most influential revenue generators and team leaders to hear the company's top leaders explain the strategy for the future, demonstrate their confidence in it and each other, and solidify a "we're all in this together" camaraderie that would have been impossible to capture in a conference call.

Utter also upped her own travel schedule and that of her management team. Traditionally, she visits each Knoll plant or regional office in the spring. In 2008, Utter and her executive team did a second tour in the autumn. "It was so important that people see me and other key leaders, and that we were honest about what was working and where the company faced risks," Utter says. Even more important was the degree of employee engagement she witnessed first-hand. "People raised their hands and asked me what they could do to help." Despite pressures to reduce travel expenses, Utter's aggressive travel schedule to connect with Knoll associates, dealers and customers continues in 2009.

DeAnne Aguirre, senior vice president at Booz & Company, notes that an increasing number of client companies have traveling executives spend time with valued local talent. "A CEO is traveling to the western region," Aguirre says. "Instead of just showing up at the regional headquarters and holding a town hall meeting, the CEO might also go with a high-performing sales or account team to visit a client." Her point: the CEO should do something that shows he or she is getting out in the field and rolling up his sleeves to help the top talent shine.

Encourage Affinity Networks

In distressing and discordant times, talented people need a home, a place to create strong bonds with their colleagues and the organization. Networking or affinity groups—grassroots, company-supported internal organizations that address the needs of a specific employee population, such as women, engineers, African Americans, or millennials—have proved a huge winner for employees and employers alike in this recession. These groups serve as secure havens for people who might otherwise feel adrift as their companies focus on survival. Affinity groups provide an outlet for employees to address what's important to them, from celebrating their heritage to building professional networks to developing career skills. Many groups also offer nuanced learning opportunities. For example, women's networks may teach negotiating skills, and millennial groups pair young members with senior mentors.

Yet many high performers don't bother to participate, either because they don't know that the groups exist or because they're not aware of their value. By reminding top talent about the customized fit of these internal networks and their comfort zone attributes, leaders can point to another way the company cares.

As the economic downturn turned into a meltdown, GE's Women's Network enhanced its circle of support for female talent with a program called My Connections. Introduced in early 2008, the program requires regional senior leaders, dubbed "champions," to sponsor local "pods"—groups of approximately twenty women who meet six to eight times a year. In addition to ensuring that up-and-coming leaders have a chance to meet other senior leaders, the pods provide much-needed personal connection during troubled times. "And that," says Deborah Elam, GE vice president and chief diversity officer, "means people do not feel so alone.

Reaching Out a Helping Hand

A massive layoff is like a death in the family. It leaves survivors shaken and unbalanced—and needing to talk. Most organizations now realize that to expect remaining star employees to pick up the pieces and soldier on as though nothing has happened is not only unrealistic but also unfeeling. A badly handled layoff can sow bitterness and rancor that will fester for years. Although there's no changing the underlying situation, showing genuine sympathy makes all the difference.

One of the most powerful actions an organization can take is to provide a safe outlet for people to vent their concerns and ask for advice. As the economic landscape shifted in 2008 and 2009, many organizations—especially those in the hard-hit financial sector—turned to their employee assistance program (EAP) for help.

Credit Suisse, for example, worked with Hewitt Associates, its benefits partner, to customize offerings that would help employees during prolonged periods of stress. They included classes on stress reduction, advice on how to live a balanced life, and even the basics of financial planning. "Many of our junior, younger employees have never lived through a deep recession and they need help recalibrating their lives," explains Kathryn Quigley.

Ironically, top performers often are not aware of the existence of EAP services, for the simple reason that they've always done so well they've never felt they needed help. The first step for many companies is alerting top talent to this resource and describing what it can do.

High-level executives and managers are under unique stress. Not only are they subjected to the same uncertainty and fear as the rank and file, but senior leaders also feel pressured to hide such feelings so that they can convey a sense of strength to peers and people under them. No one feels secure when the boss behaves in a panicky way. But keeping feelings bottled up can seriously increase stress.

At Merrill Lynch, Subha Barry, managing director and head of global diversity and inclusion, understood this, and in 2008 she orchestrated a formal event to encourage Merrill's leaders to address their stress. Barry moderated a panel of three of the firm's most seasoned and respected leaders; all had worked through the downswings and upswings of business cycles and had fashioned hugely successful careers. In front of 150 of their peers and colleagues, they openly discussed the stresses and strains that taxed them daily and talked about what they did to get themselves through rough times. One reported successfully battling an addiction to sleep medication by taking up running. Another confessed he was so depleted at the end of the day that he was "speechless" when he got home at night—unable to carry on a conversation with his wife or share the stresses of the day. Not surprisingly, this silence was damaging his marriage. Says Barry, "We wanted people to feel, 'My god, if one of the most successful leaders is standing up and talking about this, I guess it's okay for me to verbalize it too.'"

Anxiety-inducing as it is, work isn't the only source of stress for many star employees. Family responsibilities and health problems can also spike in troubled times, seeping into and exacerbating work-related stress. Sensitive employers find ways to support their best people.

In 2008 the newly formed women's employee affinity network at Moody's floated the idea of a backup child care program. When the idea was discussed at a series of companywide information sessions, however, most of the questions concerned elder care, not child care.

The company stepped up to the plate: in January 2009, dedicated centers for backup child care and elder care opened at Moody's offices in New York and San Francisco. Resources were also made available for employees in other parts of the country. "At a time when we're seeing cutbacks across the industry," says Frances Laserson, "adding *on* a benefit is an extraordinary sign of the company's commitment to employees."

Ask and Ye Shall Receive

Often, reaching out and showing humanity brings unexpected rewards.

In the middle of 2008, as the world economic outlook darkened, Mona Lau decided to reinvigorate esprit de corps at UBS by holding an internal contest. "I contacted the chairs of all the employee networks around the world [there are more than twenty] and challenged them to come up with creative ideas to motivate employees and practice our core value of being client-centric," recalls the global head of diversity and campus recruiting. "We asked people to focus on ideas that wouldn't involve a lot of money but would engage people's passions, hearts, and minds. The five top ideas would get funding and be implemented."

More than twenty proposals were submitted from all over the globe. The winning ideas included creating a social networking initiative to connect UBS employees on international assignments or traveling for business with local UBS employees, and implementing a Hong Kong-based series of workshops on career planning for children of clients and employees. This and other winning proposals are on track to become a force for good, a business development opportunity, and a retention tool for UBS.

Pay attention and treat your talented people with respect—that's what it all comes down to. As layoffs bite deeper into the payroll, the fate and future of organizations depend on the efforts of those who remain. Take care of them—and they will take care of you.

7: Re-create Pride, Purpose, and Direction

Having survived the brutal layoffs rolling through the economy, even high performers find it difficult to summon the energy and focus that were once a critical part of their professional identity. Despite the reassurance they have been given, some of your best workers will be looking for other jobs "just in case" theirs are in jeopardy. Others lose focus on what's most important and spend their time on trivial or unprofitable tasks. Still others are so consumed with fear or anger that their negative energy infects those around them.

It's no wonder that Hidden Brain Drain Task Force research found that loyalty and engagement plummeted from June 2007 to December 2008: on Wall Street—home to firms that have been hardest hit in this crisis—loyalty took a huge dive, dropping from 95 percent to 39 percent. Engagement fell from 91 percent to 65 percent.

When your stars lack commitment and engage-ment, every day feels like a forced march through quicksand. How can you help your key talent regain a firm footing?

"In tough times, it's easy for even the most dedi-cated to lose energy and second-guess their goals and direction," says Mona Lau of UBS. "You've got to get people to remember why they joined the organiza-tion in the first place."

Find the Good and Flaunt It

Employees want to feel good about their companies. They want to feel proud when they tell their friends and family where they work and what they do. In the wake of a crash, the cornerstone of any comeback plan is to refresh and reinvigorate the minds and souls of employees.

That's a tall order, especially in industries that have been hit not only by the tsunami of the global eco-nomic crisis but also with industry-specific—or even company-specific—turmoil. Still, no matter how com-plex the challenges, an important part of the solution is to emphasize the good news.

"What a leader has to do is to convey a sense of op-timism about the future," says Lisa Quiroz of Time Warner. "At a time of downsizing and restructuring, employees are hungry for success stories. At Time Warner we've all been inspired by recent triumphs at CNN. During the presidential election cycle CNN shot up in the ratings to take the number 1 slot among cable news networks, primarily due to their ability to reach a younger and more multicultural audience, in addition to keeping their core audience. By developing a strategy to reach these new audiences through more diverse talent, opinions and content on the air, as well as a more inclusive marketing strategy, CNN widened their reach considerably, particularly to African American, younger viewers. At our recent Multicultural Summit, this success was shared with senior leaders across the company—it is a big win and a source of great pride at the company."

In addition to lifting up success, talk to your high performers about the importance of the work they do. Remind them of ways in which the company's products and services benefit people outside the organization. Biotech companies have often done well on this front. At Genzyme, which specializes in therapies for rare inherited disorders, researchers routinely connect with patients whose life prospects have been greatly improved. In an interview one pathologist recounted—with great feeling—seeing a five-year-old patient who was able to run around kicking a ball after receiving treatment with a drug she had helped develop. Without that drug, the child would not have survived.

Making such heartfelt connections may not be as easy for other organizations, but simply reiterating *why* the company exists—to help clients, to serve customers—reminds disheartened employees that there's a greater purpose to their work.

This reaffirmation of a larger vision is especially relevant in recessionary times. "If you are asking people to take risks and to work harder with less prospect of reward, then give them a reason why they need to pull the stops out," says Tom Stewart of Booz & Company. "At Booz we talk about how our clients need us more than ever—and that has the virtue of also being true."

Managers can also reinspire and reinvigorate demoralized talent by finding and highlighting silver linings. Adam Quinton of Merrill Lynch stresses the learning opportunities opened up by economic downturns. "Young employees have never experienced severe economic contraction. So this is perhaps a once in a career moment—when competitors are in disarray and distracted providing the chance to up service levels, to innovate and gain an edge—something that would be much harder to do in more stable times." The message is simple: accentuate the positive, whether it's recognizing an individual's exceptional effort, noting a team's creativity in cutting costs, or acknowledging an idea for a new product or service. Share stories that remind people that they're part of a culture and an organization they can be proud of. Look for and create opportunities for good news, and don't be shy about publicizing them. "This is the time to resell and re-engage employees, especially high performers, on the company's value proposition," says Laird Post, principal at Booz & Company.

Amp Up Altruism

Tough times are precisely when not-for-profit groups (community service and arts organizations) need more than their usual level of support. Maintaining— even boosting—corporate donations is a great way for companies to stand out simply by doing the right thing. And when your top performers are working harder than ever with no promise of a raise, they want to believe that there's at least a karmic paycheck: that they are contributing to the social good. In short, when it comes to restoring employees' battered sense of pride in their organizations, charitable efforts offer a tremendous bang for the buck.

However, writing checks (or matching employees' financial contributions), although deeply appreciated, doesn't have the same effect as giving people a physical connection to doing good. In the summer of 2008, understanding that employees wanted a hands-on experience, Moody's launched a program called Afternoon of Community Service.

The volunteer program took place during the working day—a first for the company. Groups of employees volunteered for a variety of activities, including sorting fifteen hundred library books at a public school in a poor neighborhood; planting thirty-one thousand flower bulbs in a city park; lending a hand at an organization that gathers clothing for and coaches disadvantaged women going out on job interviews; and preparing lunch for 135 people at a community soup kitchen on Broadway.

Almost everyone in Moody's Corporate Finance Group (96 percent) participated in the program over a two-day period. Afterward, they were asked to answer a confidential survey about their experience. The results stunned Fran Laserson of Moody's. "We're a quantitatively focused company, our culture is not effusive or emotional. This is a group of people who rarely say *very*, yet close to 100 percent said they found the activity to be rewarding or *very* rewarding." Some 97 percent want to participate in another afternoon of community service. Sixty-seven percent built relationships with colleagues they don't usually work with. After the event 51 percent felt better about the company and 50 percent felt better about themselves.

As a follow-up, team leaders were asked to host gatherings for their groups to unpack the experience. "That was a quick win," Laserson reports. "These meetings reinforced the camaraderie that grew out of the Afternoon of Community Service, boosting morale and deepening engagement."

Recommit to Corporate Social Responsibility

There scarcely exists a corporate headquarters that doesn't boast a large piece of marble inscribed with the company credo. Often, however, these credos are dismissed as empty words. Turbulent times offer organizations an opportunity to turn fine-sounding words into concrete deeds—and, in the process, demonstrate to doubt-plagued high performers that corporate leaders care about the social bottom line as well as the financial one.

Recommitting to corporate social responsibility programs in difficult times leverages the larger purpose behind an organization's products and services. By reminding valued employees that they are part of an organization that is improving the lot of humankind, these programs deepen engagement and enhance performance.

Goldman Sachs's 10,000 Women is a case in point. Launched in March 2008, this program partners with business schools and NGOs around the world to provide training and education to selected female entrepreneurs. In addition to receiving formal training, each of the women is paired with a Goldman Sachs mentor. The mentors and mentees connect using iMentor, an online tool, which enables protégées to post questions prompted by their class work or business experiences. Mackenzie Winner, a Goldman Sachs mentor, talks about how gratifying this experience has been. "The women have been extraordinarily grateful for our help, which has truly been rewarding for me, especially when we hear that our advice has positively affected their business. It is an amazing feeling to know that you have made a positive difference in someone's life on the other side of the globe." As Goldman Sachs has weathered stormy seas on Wall Street, 10,000 Women is one of the firm's programs of public service which has helped maintain morale.

Pfizer with its Global Access program has gone one step further, incorporating altruism into its business model. The credo of this pharmaceutical giant is "working together for a healthier world." True to this mission, in September 2008, Pfizer launched the Global Access initiative, a program that is exploring ways to increase access to medicines and improve health care for the working poor in a manner that's commercially viable, socially responsible, and sustainable over the long term. One of the pilot projects is a partnership with Grameen Health which focuses on improving access and health care services provided by Grameen clinics in Bangladesh, one of the world's most populous and poorest nations.

When the program was announced, project leader Ponni Subbiah was swamped with interest. "Employees wrote to me from all functional divisions within Pfizer—research, marketing, manufacturing, operations, even the auditing group—telling me how happy they were to see Pfizer involved in this area and how it made them proud to be part of this company," says Subbiah. When Pfizer posted job openings for the internal team that would drive the program, people were so enthusiastic about the opportunity that they applied even if they didn't have the right background. Others offered to volunteer in the evenings, after work, or on weekends.

"There's a reason why we work for a health-care company and not some other organization," Subbiah explains. "We value the chance to make an impact on people's lives. Thus this Global Access initiative, which will increase access to our medicines by the working poor across the globe, feels very gratifying to us."

"People are passionate about contributing to this program," says Jean-Michel Halfon, Pfizer's president and general manager of emerging markets, adding that in his more than thirty years with the company he's never seen such a groundswell of employee enthusiasm. "People are really willing to go the extra mile and take on additional responsibilities just to be part of this program. This is a textbook case of how to turbocharge employee engagement."

Reinvent the Business Model and Point the Way Forward

At a Hidden Brain Drain strategy session at Canary Wharf, London, in June 2008, participants—who held senior positions in the banking industry—talked about how daunting it was to be working in a sector where the business model was "broken." In the words of one particularly outspoken managing director, "We know that we can't do what we've been doing any more. It's not just that mortgage-backed securities have dug us a deep hole; we simply can't leverage money in ways we've gotten used to. But where do you go from here? No one—especially the current crop of CEOs—seems to know. What is the next engine for growth? The next big money spinner? I sure wish someone would pull me in on this challenge. Involving folks on the front lines in a redesign of the business model would go some distance towards convincing me to stay at this firm."

Bankers in London are not alone. Many organizations and many sectors around the world are confronting broken business models, but some leaders are using the challenges thrown up by economic crisis—and the urgent need for innovation and strategic redirection—as opportunities to recharge and reengage top talent.

Determined to avoid the sharp blows of the 2001–2002 dot-com bust—which hit the tech sector particularly hard—John Chambers, CEO of Cisco, has taken precautionary measures. In 2007 he created (with vice president of development Annmarie Neal and senior vice president of emerging technologies Marthin De Beer) a series of high-profile "Action Learning Forums" to spearhead change in Cisco's business model. The program brings together Cisco's most outstanding talent to work in collaborative 10-person teams for three months. The 360 individuals who have participated to date cross every conceivable line—rank, function, generation, geography, and gender—but they share one thing: they are the brightest and the best, and they are being deployed to drive the next generation of innovation at the company.

The action teams are carefully structured. Hierarchal reporting relationships are thrown out the window—distinguished engineers interact on a level playing field with salespeople—and each group includes a psychologically savvy coach to facilitate team sessions. In addition, the objectives of the groups are aligned with John Chambers's top strategic priorities, ensuring that everyone pulls in the same direction. Finally, venture capital prize money is awarded to winning teams, guaranteeing that the best business plans are funded and will get off the ground.

Billions of dollars of new value creation have been generated by these teams. One idea—Smart Grid, which revamps energy grids to make them faster and more cost effective—is projected to bring in $10 billion of revenue over the next five years. There have also been impressive gains on the people front. Twenty percent of those who participated have been promoted—indeed, Cisco has lost only 2 percent of these high-potential employees since the program started. It's been an engagement and acceleration tool for the company.

When asked why Action Learning Forums have been so motivating for top talent, Neal points to "the extraordinary energy released when very capable people collaborate in an environment free of hierarchy and other artificial barriers and are told that the sky's the limit, that nothing's out of bounds." She adds, "This framework motivates people to work wonders."

Interestingly, Neal doesn't mention compensation. Financial rewards—which are hard to come by in this economic climate—are not central to the program. Some of these high flyers will get promoted, but they are giving their all right now because they believe that they're stakeholders in the future of the company and they can make a significant difference.

8: P.S. Don't Forget Yourself

"What is the first word that comes to mind when describing your day-to-day work environment?" When we asked top talent that question in Hidden Brain Drain strategy sessions, two words dominated the responses: "unbelievably stressful."

Wrestling with an extremely challenging job is difficult in the best of times. In troubled times, high performers are at risk of being knocked down, caught as they are in a three-way squeeze between clamoring clients, vaporizing value, and needy employees.

This is a serious issue because top performers provide the fuel that keeps the show on the road. Prized contributors in their own right, they are the force multipliers who motivate, encourage, and guide teams to do their best for the organization. Most of the talent management tactics we've described in this book fall on the shoulders of individuals who are stretched to their limits.

How do overloaded high performers ramp up their own resilience so that they can come through for everyone else?

The short answer is this: everything you're doing to hold on to your best people, you also should do for yourself. Even while tending to the well-being of your team and organization, you should not ignore your personal welfare.

A Vicious Cycle

There's no doubt about it: the pressures of the recession are having a measurable effect on physical health and mental well-being. Hidden Brain Drain strategy session data allows us to compare stress levels in December 2008 with those prevalent a year earlier. The result? The number of high-echelon workers reporting high levels of stress more than doubled, rising from 33 percent to 78 percent. Symptoms range from "crashing" at the end of the day (70 percent versus 43 percent six months earlier) to an "emptied out" sex life (37 percent versus 30 percent).

Participants in the research (vice presidents and managing directors—in other words, the cream of the crop) reported worrisome health issues. Some of the most common were dependence on sleep medication;

migraine headaches; anxiety attacks; immune system failure; problem drinking; and overeating.

In addition, as they deal with brutal hours in tension-filled offices, many executives can't prevent the strains at work from spilling over into their home lives, causing ill temper and spawning squabbles. With one spouse spending many hours at work, the other spouse often feels like a single parent: "It's obvious that I'm consumed by me—the company and the team—and my spouse feels cheated and overburdened with the responsibility of figuring out the home and kids for me," said one strategy session participant. Another reported "more stupid fighting as we are both stressed and tired."

With no place to hide from spiraling stress, leaders are trapped in a vicious cycle. They often end up so distracted and depleted that they can't focus on the job at hand. This is exactly what companies can least afford.

Maintain Your Equilibrium

The best advice: be hyperaware of how you react under trying circumstances, and try to correct negative behavior. "People generally have behaviors they revert to under stress," says Tom Stewart of Booz & Company. "They have something they fall back on, a coping pattern. That's why some people become thirteen again, or angry, or passive. And why others get distracted or antsy or vague."

Such behavior can sabotage your ability to lead, jeopardize your career, and taint an otherwise untarnished reputation. Stewart suggests that leaders take a personal inventory of their behavior. Try to acknowledge and stop harmful patterns. Ask yourself, "What am I doing that I can unlearn? What should I try not to do?"

Most important, you need to ask what you can do to regain and maintain your equilibrium amid the turmoil.

Exercise is probably the most obvious answer. A plethora of studies links exercise to building enduring protection from the harmful effects of stress on physical and mental health. "The single thing that comes closest to a magic bullet, in terms of strong and universal benefits, is exercise," says Frank Hu, epidemiologist at the Harvard School of Public Health. Regular workout sessions not only reduce physical and mental stress but also allow the mind to regroup. Many people say that they do their best problem solving and come up with their best ideas after exercising.

The obstacle here is failing to give yourself permission to take the time. "I work out two mornings a week," said one strategy session participant. "That causes me to get in later, but I stay later. You just have to decide that exercise is important, that you need to invest in yourself."

Give Some, Get Some

Volunteering has often been viewed as food for the soul. "If I make the time to reach out and give back, it lifts my spirits," said one strategy session participant. "Doing something for someone who has real problems," said another, "gives me a sense of perspective and reminds me that some people are in a much worse place."

It turns out that do-gooders are on to something. A recent research review conducted by Washington, D.C.-based Corporation for National & Community Service reveals that charitable work literally makes the heart grow stronger. According to this 2007 report, individuals who volunteer live longer than those who do not. For example, individuals with coronary artery disease who get involved with volunteer activities after suffering a heart attack report a reduction in despair and depression. This change of mood, in turn, drives down mortality and adds years to life. It's also true that those who volunteer have fewer incidents of heart disease in the first place.

Astoundingly, it does not require months or even weeks of charitable work to reap the health benefits of volunteering. The research shows that volunteers begin to see tangible benefits to their health by volunteering one hundred hours per year—two hours a week.

In addition, volunteering can bolster your professional well-being. Because nonprofits are perennially short on staff, they offer a golden opportunity to learn new skills in different areas, something that, in turn, will make you more valuable back in the office. Working in a not-for-profit organization is particularly helpful in developing skills in negotiation, collaboration, adaptability, and management by influence.

Nurture Your Networks

Strong personal and professional networks can be a lifeline in bad times and good. Men have famously relied on old boys networks to propel their careers—think Skull and Bones (George W. Bush), the Maidstone Club (George Soros), and the Century Club (Patrick Moynihan). In recent years women have become particularly good at creating these power tools and safety nets from scratch.

Six years ago the women partners who led the Professional Women's Network at Ernst & Young had an idea: why not create a series of events that would put top female talent at Ernst & Young together in the same room with the firm's most important female clients? The co-chair of the network, Carolyn Buck Luce, thought the way to bring this off—and make sure that two hundred extremely busy people actually showed up—was to create an intimate "salon" in New York City where senior women from all sectors could come together to talk about issues that really mattered to them as leaders and citizens. So Buck Luce and her partners set to work and "Issues on My Mind" was born. Over the years they have managed to lure the likes of Gloria Steinem, Anne Mulcahey, Andrea Jung, Kirsten Gillibrand and Donna Shalala as keynote speakers and have created a heady mix of substance and glamour. Positioned as part of E&Y's professional women's network, this quarterly dinner has become a go-to event for New York-based female business leaders. According to Buck Luce its importance has only ramped up in 2008 and 2009 as participants increasingly use it as a trust-filled venue for exploring career and business opportunities.

A recent *Harvard Business Review* article by Boris Groysberg titled "How Star Women Build Portable Skills" points out that female stars often build their franchises on external relationships. It's often easier to focus outward, where you can define the services required to succeed, than to tangle with the power structure within your own male-dominated firm. But whatever the driving force, in Groysberg's words, "the networking strategies of star women can help both men and women enhance their ability to shine in any setting." I would add, "particularly in difficult times."

Recruit a Personal Board of Directors

Companies have boards of directors, a diverse group of outside experts familiar with the company and objective enough to help chart its course. If this concept works well for organizations, why not individuals?

In December 2008 Merrill Lynch was acquired by Bank of America, and Subha Barry of Merrill knew that after the inevitable reorganization she probably would not have a job. Rather than seek out a career coach, Barry convened a personal board of directors to kick-start a job search. Her board comprised eight female executives from banking, accounting, the law, human resources, and the not-for-profit world. These women weren't necessarily her most intimate friends, but they knew Barry from leadership networks in her professional life and were loyal protagonists. They could be relied on to help identify strengths and goals, offer contacts, and provide fresh insight on a range of options.

A two-hour brainstorming session came up with three key attributes for Barry's dream job: it needed to be global and entrepreneurial, and it needed to have a mission that was both socially responsible and commercially viable. Barry's board of directors then homed in on six fields she should explore, two of which she was unfamiliar with and never would have considered on her own. To help her learn about these new fields, the board fired up their BlackBerries and put her in touch with key people. These women were willing to cash in chips on her behalf.

"Job transitions can be extremely lonely," Barry told me, "but now I have a sense of security because there is a group of people I can lean on. I have more clarity of thought, because this group helped me define my goals more quickly than I could have done myself. I particularly appreciate access to their connections. Even though this is a terrible marketplace, I have no doubt that I will find a great job."

Restore and Reflect

There's a belief out there that great leaders need always to be on and on call.

It's a myth.

Everyone—especially CEOs—needs time out to tend body and soul and gain fresh perspectives. How can you beat back the stressors of your job and build physical resilience if you don't take an occasional holiday? And how can you figure out where the world is going—and what the next round of innovation needs to look like—if you don't take chunks of time for considered reflection?

Bill Gates has always claimed that the success he achieved in leading Microsoft was based, in large measure, on the time he took out of a packed schedule to reflect and think. During the years he was at the helm at Microsoft, he set aside one week twice a year for quiet reflection—to mull over global trends, to read and digest a range of new knowledge. He fiercely protected these "think weeks," and they were largely free of distractions; friends, family, and Microsoft employees were banned. Looking back, Gates sees these periods of quiet reflection as contributing greatly to his ability to anticipate, innovate—and lead.

This brings us to a final word of wisdom: as pressures mount in this brutal global recession, don't turn the screws, don't whip yourself into a frenzy of activity. Give yourself the same advice you give to your best people. Take time and take care.

Conclusion:
Becoming a Talent Magnet

I've said it before, but it's worth repeating: a recession is a terrible thing to waste.

The menu of pragmatic interventions highlighted in this book jump-starts a winning strategy, giving companies a rare opportunity to gain powerful advantage in the marketplace. Valuing people and turbocharging performance are important at any point in the economic cycle but are critical during a recession. Being known as a standout employer during a brutal and prolonged downturn has an enduring impact on a company's image and reputation, enabling it to attract and retain the brightest and the best over the long haul.

There are lessons from the 2001 dot-com bust. Cisco's response was to offer high-potential employees alternatives to layoffs (leadership sabbaticals and the like), a move that burnished its employer brand and positioned the company for takeoff into a next highly successful phase of growth. John Chambers understood that holding on to Cisco's high-octane brainpower was key to the company's renewal. After all, where else were the great new products and smart marketing ideas going to come from?

Reputation and Employer Brand

Reputation is in the news as we watch once-proud firms like AIG being brought down by bad judgment and out-of-control greed, forever sullying the names of executives associated with them. Financial services firms are at the center of the meltdown. In early 2009 Congressman Barney Frank, chairman of the House Financial Services Committee, summed up popular sentiment when he told a group of Wall Street executives, "People really hate you." Such is the pariah status of the financial sector that one retired executive confessed, "I'd almost rather say I work in pornography."

If ever there was a time when we need to understand the importance of reputation—and brand—this is it.

A strong employer brand that recognizes the value of top talent and creates the conditions that allow talent to flourish is a huge differentiator. Not only does a strong brand spur renewal and growth, but also it sets your company up to be a talent magnet—an employer of choice in what will become an increasingly competitive labor market.

Demographic Drivers

Make no mistake about it: although the underlying mismatch between the demand and supply of top-notch people is currently obscured by global recession, demographic trends are on course to produce a talent crunch in the not-so-distant future.

In mature economies there are serious concerns about the size of Gen X (now aged thirty-one through forty-four), which turns out to be a very small generation. In the United States, for example, it's only forty-six million strong, a little more than half the size of the baby boom generation. If this is the bench strength for leadership—and of course it is—companies have reason to be worried that soon there won't be enough leaders to go around.

In emerging markets the presenting problem is the size of Gen Y (ages fifteen to thirty). In the BRIC economies (Brazil, Russia, India, and China), because of baby busts and plummeting birthrates, Gen Y has 40 percent fewer people than the preceding generation. This shortage is particularly worrisome for global companies, because many see the BRIC economies as providing the best prospects for growth and expansion in the near term.

The bottom line: an employer brand that lures young talent by dint of delivering an extraordinary value proposition is essential for competitive strength going forward.

If any company knows how to do this, it's Google; in 2008 the company ranked first on the *Fortune* (U.S.) list of best companies to work for, and first on the *Financial Times* (U.K.) list of best workplaces.

Google Points the Way

Google has won global renown for cutting-edge innovation and for its leadership role in the democratization of information. Yet a large part of its brand strength rests upon the hugely attractive—and distinctive—value proposition it offers to employees.

TGIF (Thank God It's Friday) is a weekly, company-wide get-together started by Google cofounders Larry Page and Sergey Brin. Once a week, a senior executive leads a global TGIF in front of a group of employees, usually at Google's Mountain View, California, headquarters. The meeting is posted online and archived for those who can't log on in real time. Although TGIF includes standard corporate communication—the presiding senior executive welcomes new employees and shares Google-related happenings—the highlight by far is the Q&A session. Employees submit questions through e-mail or take the microphone in person. According to the Great Places to Work Institute which has named Google #1 on the list of 100 Best Companies to Work For, the session reflects a belief that employees should feel comfortable asking even the most senior members of the management team tough questions, and that executives should talk with employees as openly as possible. No question is off-limits. Questions range from "What are Google's growth rate projections" to why Google wasn't the default search engine in Opera Mini. The events are so valued that some of Google field offices have taken to hosting their own TGIFs.

It's a philosophy, not a policy. If a company has a culture where open dialogue and information sharing is encouraged and respected, then there will be no need for formal programs—like focus groups that mine opinion, or blogs that tell employees what the CEO is thinking, or expensive brochures that tell employees what they may need to hear—because everyone's thoughts and feelings come out during the course of daily interaction and the weekly Q&A. The dialogue itself is the program. Employees may not like all the answers, but hopefully they will appreciate the fact that they are able to raise the questions.

An open approach to talent management has been a hallmark of the Google brand since its founding, as have amazing employee perks, ranging from on-site massage and gourmet food to creative work arrangements that allow employees to spend 20 percent of their time on noncore activities—thinking and working outside the box, driving the next generation of innovation. All this has helped Google gain access to an exceptionally rich talent pool—it receives a thousand applications for each job opening—and has catapulted the company to the top of best-company-to-work-for lists around the world.

Unpacking the complex alchemy that creates a knock-your-socks-off brand is a difficult task, but one thing is clear: many of the action steps highlighted in this book are at the center of the Google strategy. TGIF is all about creating a no-spin zone (intervention 1), and allowing employees to spend time on their own ideas is all about providing meaningful nonmonetary rewards (intervention 3).

Low-Hanging Fruit and the Bottom Line

Google and other standout employer brands are unusual. In most companies talent is distressingly disengaged; across a broad swath of the economy, rather few employees are committed to their work.

The data is startling. In 2008 consulting firm Towers Perrin looked at engagement rates across eighteen geographies and found that a mere 21 percent of respondents worldwide were fully engaged with their jobs—willing to go the extra mile to help their organizations succeed. A new study by Modern Survey shows that although 27 percent of employees are moderately engaged, only 12 percent are fully engaged.

Particularly troubling is that the current global economic crisis seems to be triggering a further drop in engagement—and performance. As we have seen, Hidden Brain Drain research shows a sharp decline in engagement among high-echelon workers between June 2007 and December 2008, with engagement levels falling 12 percent on Main Street and 26 percent on Wall Street, underscoring urgency of the challenge.

The only silver lining here is that if the current low rates of employee engagement can be turned around, there's a huge upside in productivity gains that go straight to the bottom line.

A slew of research demonstrates a strong positive link between employee engagement and productivity. A recent study (again by Towers Perrin) across fifty global companies shows that raising employee engagement creates a 14 percent increase in net income. The Corporate Leadership Council has undertaken similar research; it looked at engagement levels for fifty thousand employees around the world and found that employees who are engaged outperform those who are not by 20 percent. In short, there's a significant payoff when companies are able not only to lure top talent but also to support and inspire these high-octane individuals (women and men) so that they fire on all cylinders.

There are few guarantees in these uncertain times. But one thing is certain: only by reengaging your talented employees and instituting management practices that turbocharge their brainpower will you have both the ideas and the commitment to overcome adversity, flourish in prosperity, and continue to attract smart people for years to come. In the words of James S. Turley, CEO of Ernst & Young, "In a down market, leveraging your talent to create competitive advantage is more important than ever."

Notes

1. The Hidden Brain Drain Task Force was founded in February 2004 by Sylvia Ann Hewlett (Center for Work-Life Policy and Columbia University), Carolyn Buck Luce (Ernst & Young) and Cornel West (Princeton University) to help corporations leverage their talent across the divides of gender, generation and culture. Comprised of senior leaders from fifty global corporations, the task force represents 4 million employees in 152 countries. Members are united by an understanding that the full utilization of the talent pool is at the heart of competitive advantage and economic success. The Hidden Brain Drain Task Force has completed five major research studies and helped seed more than seventy best practices.

2. Sylvia Ann Hewlett and Carolyn Buck Luce, "Extreme Jobs: The Dangerous Allure of the 70-Hour Workweek," *Harvard Business Review*, December 2006.

3. 2006 data is derived from two Center for Work-Life Policy surveys: a U.S. survey of 1,564 high-income employees (844 men and 720 women) and a global survey of 975 managers at large multinational companies (652 men and 323 women). For more detail, see *Seduction and Risk: The Emergence of Extreme Jobs* (New York: Center for Work-Life Policy, 2007).

The 2007 and 2008 data is derived from a series of focus groups and Virtual Strategy Sessions (VSSs)—a proprietary research tool of the Center for Work-Life Policy. Virtual Strategy Sessions comprise innovative "virtual" focus groups designed to facilitate participatory group discussion and brainstorming through simultaneous online and voice communications. Qualified participants in the sessions were high-potential employees (junior and senior, running the gamut from manager to vice president, from analyst to managing director) who worked in companies identified as "Wall Street" and "Main Street." A total of 266 men and women took part in the focus groups and strategy sessions.

January 2009 data is derived from a Center for Work-Life Policy demographic survey of 1,046 U.S. male and female college graduates.

4. "Sustaining High Performance in Difficult Times: A Special Report" is available at http://harvardbusiness.org/.

5. Data in this paragraph comes from Sylvia Ann Hewlett, *Off-Ramps and On-Ramps* (Harvard Business School Press, 2007).

About the Author

Sylvia Ann Hewlett is an economist and the founding president of the Center for Work-Life Policy (CWLP), a nonprofit think tank, where she chairs the "Hidden Brain Drain," a task force of fifty global companies and organizations committed to fully realizing female and multicultural talent. In addition, she directs the Gender and Policy Program at the School of International and Public Affairs, Columbia University. She is a member of the World Economic Forum's Global Agenda Council on the Gender Gap.

Hewlett is the author of six *Harvard Business Review* articles and nine critically acclaimed nonfiction books, including *When the Bough Breaks* (Basic Books, winner of a Robert F. Kennedy Memorial Book Prize) and *Off-Ramps and On-Ramps* (Harvard Business School Press, named as one of the best business books of 2007 by Amazon.com). Her writings have appeared in the *New York Times,* the *Financial Times, Foreign Affairs, Veja,* and the *International Herald*

Tribune. She is a featured blogger, appearing monthly on Harvard Business Online and ForbesWoman.com.

Hewlett is the founder of Sylvia Ann Hewlett Associates LLC, a boutique consultancy. In 2009 Sylvia Ann Hewlett Associates formed an alliance with Booz & Company, focused on helping organizations leverage top talent across the divides of culture, gender, and generation.

Hewlett is a well-known speaker on the international stage. She has keynoted International Women's Day at the IMF, given the featured address at Pfizer's Emerging Markets Leadership Summit in Dubai, and spoken at the White House with coauthor Cornel West. She is a frequent guest on TV and radio, appearing on *Oprah, NewsHour with Jim Lehrer, Charlie Rose, ABC World News Tonight, The Today Show, The View, BBC World News,* and *Talk of the Nation*—and she has been lampooned on *Saturday Night Live.*

A Kennedy Scholar and graduate of Cambridge University, Hewlett earned her PhD in economics at London University.